GOD'S TRUTH ABOUT AMERICA!

A Sequel To: *Our Crumbling Foundation –*
Will God Cancel Us?

By Mist Carter

Assent Books

Updated Edition 2023

ISBN:978-1-938814-40-2

DEDICATION

First and foremost, I want to thank God for blessing me with His gifts, guidance, and grace. I dedicate this book to my family and friends on earth and in heaven, as well as my fellow patriots. I want to especially thank my friend and amazingly talented artist, Kathy Radich, who not only designed the book cover but encouraged me in the process of writing both of my books. Let's all do our part to share God's truth about America!

TABLE OF CONTENTS

PROLOGUE

My previous book, *Our Crumbling Foundation – Will God Cancel Us?* was written about a month after President Biden was sworn into office. In very short order, it was crystal clear that our nation was being dismantled before our very eyes. So much happened in such a short period of time it was hard to fathom what was occurring, as well as the negative impact that would result. The destruction to our nation is even more dangerous now, so I had to write a sequel.

During the previous administration under President Trump, America was thriving economically and militarily, had illegal immigration under control, had secure borders, was respected globally, had healthy and fair trade agreements, was energy independent, passed the Criminal Justice Reform Bill, unemployment rates for African, Asian, Hispanic, and female Americans fell to record lows, reduced the number of Americans off of food stamps by 4.6 million, historic tax cuts assisted American families and workers, American manufacturing increased, held China, Russia, Iran, and North Korea in check, reduced prescription drug prices, signed the "Right to Try" legislation for terminally ill patients, secured funding to fight the opioid epidemic, adopted programs and funding to fight crime including MS-13 gangs, successfully had other nations of NATO increase their funding, total commitment to the care of our veterans, reimposed sanctions on Iran nuclear deal, appointed numerous federal judges and two Supreme Court Justices, and rolled back burdensome and costly government regulations to benefit businesses and families. This is only a partial list of the positive accomplishments of Trump's administration, but you get the idea.

Sadly, the Biden administration started to undo nearly all of these beneficial achievements on day one, and most of this was motivated by the hate of Donald Trump. Yet, it just wasn't Biden and his cronies who were the only culprits responsible for the socialist takeover of our nation. It was also fueled and promoted through the lying propaganda of most of our media outlets.

"Good people hate what is false, but the wicked do shameful and disgraceful things" (Proverbs 13:5, NCV).

> All day long you plot destruction. Your tongue cuts like a sharp razor; you're an expert at telling lies. You love evil more than good and lies more than truth. You love to destroy others with your words, you liar!
>
> Psalm 52:2-4 (NLT)

In this sequel, we will re-visit many of the topics addressed in the previous book and see if we have progressed or regressed in restoring our nation to the godly standards on which it was founded.

"Everyone who hears my words and obeys them is like a wise man who built his house on rock" (Matthew 7:24, NCV).

There are all types of structures and houses in the world. Big or small, beautiful or plain, elaborate or humble. It doesn't matter what style it is; what is crucial is the foundation upon which it stands. The same holds true for nations and governments, as it does for houses. It is paramount that the foundation is unshakeable. Our country was the first and only country in history that was founded on a brand-new idea: the idea that people have rights.

These rights are the right to one's own life (which includes that which one has worked for), the right to one's own liberty (freedom to live the way you want—provided you don't hurt anyone else), and the right to pursue one's own happiness (not everyone else's—yours). The purpose of government was to only do that one thing and nothing else. It was to protect these God-given individual rights.

Christian values, morals, and principles were an integral component of our nation's foundation and underlay some key tenets of America's constitutional order. For instance, the founders believed that humans are created in the image of God, which led them to design institutions and laws meant to protect and promote human dignity. When George Washington placed his hand on a Bible to take the oath of office, it wasn't merely a formality but a declaration that the Bible would be the ultimate source of wisdom and guidance for his administration. He once said, "It is impossible to rightly govern the world without God and the Bible."

So, let's examine where we are as a nation. Let's expose the fierce and constant efforts of those on the extreme left and their sidekicks in the mainstream media, who are executing to undermine and destroy our nation and its firm foundation. Yet, it doesn't stop by simply exposing these facts; we must stop allowing this ruination of our republic to continue and instead fight back hard.

"Fight the good fight for the true faith."
(1 Timothy 6:12, NLT)

CHAPTER ONE

$-\,-\,-\,§\,-\,-\,-$

God's Truth

Let's take a moment to address truth (God's truth), lies, and semantics in today's America. Merriam-Webster defines "truth" as (1) "the body of real things, events, and facts: Actuality; (2) the state of being the case: Fact; and (3) a transcendent fundamental or spiritual reality."

Scripture provides us with numerous examples to declare that God is truth. This fact is a shining portrayal of one of God's magnificent and constant attributes. Here are a few of these declarative verses found in God's Word:

"Your kingdom is built on what is right and fair. Love and truth are in all you do" (Psalm 89:14, NCV).

"All of your words are truth. Every one of your righteous ordinances endures forever" (Psalm 119:160, WEB).

"Jesus told him, 'I am the way, the truth, and the life. No one can come to the Father except through me'" (John 14:6, NLT).

Sadly, we humans possess a sinful nature. As believers, we sometimes cling to God's truth and try to have it guide our daily lives. Unfortunately, we aren't always successful in following that guidance. Most times, we are made aware of our untruthfulness through God's Holy Spirit. When we pay heed to these revelations, we can choose to hold on to our lie or come clean and make amends for our lack of candor.

"Good people will be guided by honesty; dishonesty will destroy those who are not trustworthy" (Proverbs 11:3, NCV).

On the other end of the spectrum, those who choose not to follow God's truth are blind and deaf to facing the error of their ways and instead fall deeper into the rabbit hole of deception. They are often influenced by power, money, and/or pure evil. They manipulate the truth through distortion and/or omission of actual events. Does this sound familiar? You guessed it; this is in the job descriptions for numerous media outlets, politicians, governmental agencies, and Big Tech companies. In fact, God's Word calls out these individuals and groups in the Bible with Scripture verses such as:

"They will stop listening to the truth and will begin to follow false stories" (2 Timothy 4:4, NCV).

"But for those who are self-seeking and who reject the truth and follow evil, there will be wrath and anger" (Romans 2:8, NIV).

Perhaps every generation has thought at some point that they were living in very dark times. We could certainly say the same about the current state of our nation. In what seems like warp speed, America has allowed evil and lawlessness to become a dominant force of influence. The further away we move from our founding on godly principles and the wisdom and truth of His Word, our chances of overcoming these dark times grow dimmer.

"The way of the good person is like the light of dawn, growing brighter and brighter until full daylight. But the wicked walk around in the dark; they can't even see what makes them stumble" (Proverbs 4:18–19, NCV).

"All who do evil hate the light and will not come to the light, because it will show all the evil things they do" (John 3:20, NCV).

The Book of Proverbs in the Bible is a spiritual recipe book on how to live a life that God intended for us to live—before sin came into the picture. These proverbs can guide us to discern between good and evil and navigate through this life in a truthful, disciplined, and spirit-filled manner.

"Fear of the LORD is the foundation of wisdom" (Proverbs 9:10, NLT).

"Learn the truth and never reject it. Get wisdom, self-control, and understanding" (Proverbs 23:23, NCV).

The antonym of truth is a "lie," which is defined as "an untrue or inaccurate statement, used to deceive." The political world is infiltrated by semantics, which has become a big contributor to these restless and divisive times in which we live. In some cases, the very definition of a word has evolved to mean whatever the ideology from where it came wants it to mean; regardless if it differs from an actual definition, a dictionary states that it means. Let's look at a couple of examples of the semantical differences between dictionary definitions and the radical left.

Semantics of Racism

Merriam-Webster defines the word "racism" as "a belief that race *is a fundamental* determinant *of human traits and capacities and that racial differences produce an inherent superiority of a particular race.*" But that definition has now changed to state that non-whites are incapable of being racist, while whites are automatically racist. A couple of quotes from Thomas Sowell, a black author, address racism in this manner:

"The word 'racism' is like ketchup. It can be put on practically anything – and demanding evidence makes you a 'racist.'"

"Racism is not dead, but it is on life support – kept alive by politicians, race hustlers and people who get a sense of superiority by denouncing others as 'racists.'"

According to the left, everything is racist. The list is extensive, but here are a few examples, as ridiculous as they are, of what the left considers to be racist: all white men, police officers, "God Bless America," voter ID laws, Aunt Jemima syrup, math, Dumbo the elephant, Dr. Seuss books, the National Anthem, the Constitution, and let's not forget conservatism (regardless of the fact that people of all colors, races, and ethnicities ascribe to conservative values), and walls or fences (despite the fact that President Biden put up a tax-payer funded wall to protect his vacation home in Delaware, and Nancy Pelosi ordered a fence to be erected around the Capitol grounds following the incident on January 6, 2021).

Since the left considers everything that does not support their ideology and agenda to be racist and that whites are the only humans that are racist, then why has the left expanded that label to be placed on nearly everything—inanimate or not? When America experienced a lot more real examples of true racism in the mid-twentieth century, the label of racism was more akin to the actual dictionary definition. This overuse and abuse of the term racist have rendered it almost meaningless.

Semantics of Tolerance

Another example of a word that has been overused and misused semantically is "tolerance." The dictionary defines the word "tolerance" as "the ability or willingness to tolerate or allow the existence of opinions or behavior that one does not necessarily agree with." Some synonyms of tolerance include open-mindedness, patience, endurance, etc. Yet, in the past several years, the semantics of the word tolerance has transitioned to mean something different from the original definition. Nowadays, to lack tolerance toward the belief and/or behavior of another person is to demonstrate intolerance *of* that person. Well, wait a minute. Isn't that the description of bigotry? This misuse and abuse of the term tolerance are actually as intolerant as the intolerance it detests.

This destruction of tolerance results in people who hold opinions or beliefs that differ from another's being shamed, ostracized, or canceled. This is a call to stop this madness and return to the true definition and practice of tolerance. It is possible to hold a difference of opinion while showing respect toward those with whom we differ. Academics no longer invite disagreement and debate. Incivility reigns in the public square. In an age that preaches tolerance, intolerance has gained the upper hand.

There are several more examples of political semantics where the left is trying to change or misuse the meanings of words or phrases. It is unfortunate that numerous media outlets and numerous elected political leaders at all levels of government fail to disclose the truth, omit the truth, and/or distort the truth. As frustrating as these antics are, we need to hold firmly to our faith in God and that His truth is the only truth that matters.

God's Truth about Racism and Tolerance

God does not favor one culture over another. There are many scriptures that speak of God's love for the world, of Christ coming to be the Savior of the world, and of the Spirit's work in the world that remind us that God is not favoring any one group with the gospel message. He loves every ethnic group. He loves without discrimination. Christ came for every people, group, and race. Some verses in the Bible emphasize that to treat anyone in a discriminatory manner based on social, economic, or racial factors is to dishonor God.

"But if you favor some people over others, you are committing a sin. You are guilty of breaking the law" (James 2:9, NLT).

"For God does not show favoritism" (Romans 2:11, NLT).

"It's God's own truth, nothing could be plainer: God plays no favorites! It makes no difference who you are or where you're from—if you want God and are ready to do as he says, the door is open" (Acts 10:34-36, MSG).

It is certainly apparent that most media outlets do not share God's perspective on racism. In fact, it's quite the opposite. The media promotes racism by focusing on videos that show hatred between different races. It rarely promotes videos that show how many people from different races interact with each other in welcoming and loving ways. The media is out to maximize its own bottom line; it's not out to maximize our enlightenment. It wants people to tune in, gain ad revenue, and seize power. To get what it wants, it has to sell a story and stir controversy. It knows that "White Cop Kills White Man" won't get anyone up in arms. People are killed every day in one way or another, and we're pretty much numb to it. It really doesn't faze us. Racism, on the other hand, is a hot topic. Racism sells. So if the headline reads "Another Black Man Killed by White Cops"—now that makes for a great story.

The media is controlled by the elite: power-hungry individuals who want us to hate each other. The elite knows that racism makes it difficult for people to unite against them. Thus, they promote racial discrimination—through the media—because it guarantees them power. The media is in the business of pouring out lies, distorting the truth, and omitting the facts.

> "Stand your ground, putting on the belt of truth and the
> body armor of God's righteousness."
> (Ephesians 6:14, NLT)

CHAPTER TWO
--- § ---

Economy and Inflation:
How Can You Spend What You Don't Have?

It's getting harder and harder to trust individuals and institutions these days. This especially is the case when it comes to those we elect to political positions and those who play major roles in governmental agencies. The primary duty of these officials is to serve the people. During the election process, politicians make endless promises, many upon which they will not or cannot deliver. However, there are a handful of elected officials that do operate with sound integrity. Unfortunately, those few individuals are often mocked by the media and those who live by the new definition of being tolerant, demonstrating an intolerance of people with integrity.

Most of the elected politicians and those appointed officials to the federal government seem to be out of touch with reality. Or, it may just be that they are not being truthful. Politicians, bureaucrats, and Federal Reserve officials have long been lying to the public. They manipulate the statistics to fit their agenda, and the media compliantly supplies the headlines about these false statistics. Either the media elites are economic illiterates, or they have an agenda to sell. It's probably a little of both. Regardless, the statistics and how they are gathered go unquestioned.

Inflation is here, and it's very real. The government uses a formula called the consumer price index (CPI) to determine inflation rates. However, this CPI formula is fudged by the FED and misreported to keep the issue of inflation off the public radar. We can't print our way to prosperity. Printing too much money, as the government has done, has led us to inflation. Prosperity is a result of a nation being productive. But the government is putting forth its toughest effort by restricting productive pursuits like work and education due to the unrealistic and non-science-based COVID-19 restrictions. We'll get to that later.

As mentioned, the Federal Reserve is a big culprit to the inflation problem by printing massive amounts of money to purchase government debt and to keep interest rates artificially low. These low-interest rates result in increased prices causing individuals to actually pay more for houses, cars, and other products. The low rates allow corporations and government entities to run up our debt and pretend the rising debt is not dangerous.

The FED has printed over $9 trillion since September 2019. Federal Chairman Jerome Powell and Treasury Secretary Janet Yellen describe the situation as "transitory inflation." They, along with Biden, won't dare look into the mirror and own up to the fact that their policies, mandates, and manipulative tricks have led to this inflation. And the corporate media supports (and hides from the public) these deceptive practices.

Biden claims he inherited a bad and weak economy. That is not completely truthful. The Trump administration had truly made America great again economically until the COVID-19 pandemic hit. The US economy reached a peak in monthly economic growth in February 2020. This was the longest recorded US expansion, which began in June 2009. Sadly, that came to an end when the China Virus changed everything.

What was supposed to be a short-term measure to get a handle on the pandemic turned out to do more harm economically and end the gains the Trump administration had created. Between March and April 2020, forty-three out of fifty states issued stay-at-home orders, as well as temporary closures of non-essential businesses. All Democrat governors (twenty-four) issued these orders, while only nineteen of the twenty-six Republican governors did the same. The red states kept their stay-at-home orders in effect for thirty to forty-five days, while the blue states kept theirs in place anywhere from one month to as many as eight months. States with the most restrictive policies had substantially more unemployment than states with the least restrictive policies.

COVID-19 related job losses wiped out one hundred thirteen straight months of job growth, with total nonfarm employment falling by 20.5 million jobs in April of 2020. Consumer spending saw very sharp declines in restaurant spending, air travel, small business growth, and goods and services while spending increased in the grocery sector due to the mad dash to stockpile toilet paper. There wasn't much time to squeeze the Charmin when it was flying off the shelves.

The COVID-19 crisis has damaged the nation's industrial production output in the manufacturing, mining, and energy sectors. US industrial production dropped sharply in March 2020 as a result of the lockdowns and has since only partially rebounded. This decline posed a host of challenges for the US manufacturing sector, which employs nearly 13 million workers.

But the states and businesses that were willing to actually follow the real science, instead of the fear-mongering constantly spewed out by almighty Fauci, helped to see some improvement in the third and fourth quarters of 2020. Unfortunately, Congress kept extending the Unemployment Compensation program under the CARES Act of March 2020.

Through the Pandemic Unemployment Assistance (PUA) program, the CARES Act expanded the list of eligible recipients, adding those who would not typically be eligible for unemployment insurance. Workers were then eligible to receive state unemployment benefits as well as the extra $600 per week. Those benefits were originally due to expire on July 31, 2020. But, perverted Pelosi and her brood of vipers extended these benefits through September 6, 2021.

In 2020–2021 there were three stimulus packages, which had very little going into the hands of those who needed it most. Sadly, but not surprising, the Secret Service revealed in December 2021 that nearly $100 billion at minimum had been stolen from COVID-19 relief programs through unemployment insurance and loan fraud. Perhaps if the almighty Fauci hadn't wielded his undue power to keep America shut down for months and months, there wouldn't have been a need to do three relief packages and make unemployment benefits more lucrative than what one would earn by working, there would have been less dollar loss due to fraud. As a result of the pandemic shutdowns, many small businesses had to close permanently. Restaurants and other small businesses that were allowed to re-open couldn't find enough workers to keep their businesses operating at full capacity. This, of course, was due to these workers opting to sit at home and receive (not earn) magnified unemployment benefits that were more than their wages would have amounted to had they gone back to work.

Restaurants were especially hard-hit and continue to have challenges, especially in Democrat-run cities and states. Much of this has to do with the ridiculous mandates to wear the decorative face coverings called masks. Come on, really? We walk into the restaurant, get seated, and *then* we can remove our masks. Boy, that COVID-19 virus is as sharp as a marble. It knows not to infect you while seated at a table. Amazing! We'll address masking later in the book—I can't wait.

The middle class bears the brunt of inflation through rising food, energy, and other prices. Then later, when the government tries to ignore rising inflation and instead imposes higher taxes, the middle class will see its income squeezed even more. The corporate media pushes the Build Back Better plan, which mainly supports the far-left socialist agenda. Don't you think it should be called the *Broke By Billions* plan instead?

Main-stream media outlets rarely talk about the causes of inflation. But when they do, they somehow miss the gorilla in the room: energy policies. On the first day of his presidency, Biden set out to destroy oil companies and reduce production. This policy alone has contributed significantly to the price spike in energy prices—and those high prices flow through the entire economy as they affect all prices. The high energy prices especially harm the poor, middle class, and small businesses, about whom the media and other Democrats pretend to care. If Biden and the Democrats focus on the destruction of the fossil fuel industry, without scientific evidence, the price spikes will not be transitory as they claimed in mid-2021— they will intensify.

What about the rising cost of fuel? The twenty to thirty dollars extra people have to spend to fill their tank is having a major impact on families, as well as businesses. It will cost an extra thousand dollars this winter to heat our homes. If trucking fuel prices go up, the prices of the products they are transporting go up. You don't need a Harvard MBA to figure that out. Have you been to a grocery store lately? Do you think Pete Buttigieg can put the diaper down to figure out that destroying our energy independence caused the chaos in our supply chain?

Biden and others continue with their shameless lies that Build Back Better will lower inflation, that no one making under $400,000 will see taxes rise, and the bill will be fully funded. Neither members of Congress nor the public really knows what is in the bill. In fact, jabbering Jen Psaki was recently quoted in a briefing to the press, "They don't know exactly what's in Build Back Better and what it means. And it's always easier to sell a package to the public once it's passed." The media knows the propaganda about this bill by Biden and his cronies is not factual, yet that does not block them from spreading the misinformation. They never blocked anyone from spreading the Russian disinformation, now did they? Can you still say inflation is transitory?

So, did Biden inherit a bad and weak economy? To an extent, he did. Had he taken office, let's say, in May 2020, he would have definitely inherited a very troubling economy because of his own doing. But when he was actually sworn in on January 20, 2021, our economy had rebounded fairly significantly. In other words, it was better when he did take office than it was twelve months later.

But of course, the corporate media won't share with their viewers how grim our economy has become as a result of the socialist policies of the Biden administration. They are, however, at least starting to report on bits and pieces of what is actually happening. That's because they are personally being affected by inflation and a weak economy. Yet, they won't address the causes of such. Would you expect them to?

God's Truth about the Economy and Inflation

As previously mentioned, the Book of Proverbs in the Bible is a spiritual recipe book on how to live a life of integrity. The Bible is also full of verses that address money and economic dealings. First and foremost, we need to realize a couple of truths from God.

"The Lord God placed the man in the Garden of Eden to tend and watch over it" (Genesis 1:27, NLT).

"The earth belongs to the Lord, and everything in it—the world and all its people" (Psalm 24:1, NCV).

We are given the privilege of being good stewards of all that God created. Included in that stewardship responsibility is taking care of the economy. Sadly, our economic system has been tainted by creating a huge budget deficit, implementing immoral wealth transfers, and enabling one generation to live beyond its means only to pass that debt to the next generation.

Not only are we created in God's image and able to control the economic system, but we are also sinful and too often follow the path of greed and exploitation. When we use the Bible as our framework, we can begin to construct a government and an economy that liberates human potentiality and limits human sinfulness.

The Book of Hosea in the Old Testament states:

> But you must return to your God; maintain love and justice, and wait for your God always. The merchant uses dishonest scales and loves to defraud. Ephraim boasts, 'I am very rich; I have become wealthy. With all my wealth they will not find in me any iniquity or sin.'
>
> Hosea 12:6–8 (NIV)

The message here is that the successful but unscrupulous mercantile class of Ephraim (Israel) had become Canaan; that is, a people who were as unethical as the original Canaanites. These people believed that their wealth and connections had put them out of reach of prosecution; they had acquired the status of being above the law. The merchant's assertion was not, "With all my wealth they will not find in me any iniquity or sin," but, "With all my wealth they will not find in me any iniquity for which I can be held accountable." The point is that although they may escape retribution within the justice system of Israel, they will not escape God's retribution—nor will we.

Because humans are sinful and selfish, some people will abuse the capitalist system to feed their greed. But that is not so much an attack on capitalism as it is an understanding of the human condition. The objective of capitalism is not to change people but to protect them from human sinfulness. When utilized correctly, capitalism is a system in which bad people can do the least harm, and good people can have the freedom to do good works. Capitalism works well if you have completely moral individuals. But it doesn't function adequately when you have selfish and greedy people in charge.

Other economic systems like socialism ignore the biblical definitions of human nature. Thus, they allow economic power to be centralized and reserve power in the hands of a few greedy people. Those who complain of the influence that major corporations have on our lives should consider the socialist alternative of how a few governmental bureaucrats control every aspect of their lives. We don't want this now, do we? We must bring God back into not only our economic affairs but every aspect of our lives.

> "I will give them hearts that recognize me as the LORD. They will be my people, and I will be their God, for they will return to me wholeheartedly." (Jeremiah 24:7, NLT)

CHAPTER THREE
— — —§— — —

The Truth and Myths about COVID-19: Fauci—
The Vaccine Villain!

Nobody denies that COVID-19 is real and can be fatal to those who have vulnerable health risk factors. Is there only one weapon we should use to deal with it? Should there be only one (non-elected) bureaucrat dictating how we should fight this pandemic? Are vaccines that were developed at warp speed our only option or choice? The answer to these questions is a big fat no!

How has one man, fascist Fauci, become God? There's no disputing his education and experience in the research of infectious diseases, as well as being appointed director of the NIAID (National Institute of Allergy and Infectious Diseases) in 1984. He has served in that position under seven presidents. Fauci has been front and center concerning previous outbreaks of diseases in the past but rose to his illustrious throne since the COVID-19 pandemic has consumed America and other parts of the world. He has been admired and loved by some, but truth-seekers aren't fooled by his title, his throne, or his endless appearances on corporate media outlets. Americans have seen Fauci on TV more than the "My Pillow" ads.

Aldous Huxley, the author of *Brave New World*, had some interesting quotes that are applicable today. One of them states, "You shall know the truth, and the truth shall make you mad."

Well, Americans are finally waking up to the truth, and yes, we are beyond mad! Another Huxley quote, which is fitting for this chapter, is: "The men the American people admire most extravagantly are the most daring liars; the men they detest most violently are those who try to tell them the truth." This pretty much describes Fauci, the Biden administration, and the mainstream media.

The real truth about the vaccine villain, and his sordid past, is meticulously exposed in Robert Kennedy Jr.'s best-selling book *The Real Anthony Fauci*. Despite being number one on Amazon's best seller list, the media launched a blackout campaign to downplay the existence of the book. I strongly recommend you read this amazing exposure of how Fauci and his puppeteer, Bill Gates, have made billions of dollars through deceptive measures that cost thousands of lives under the guise of trying to save lives. The main tactic used was *fear*. Kennedy describes the collaborative efforts of big pharma, mainstream media, and government bureaucrats to abuse pandemics and/or pseudo-pandemics to control the population and achieve tyrannical power.

I'm not going to spell out all the gory details about how the repeated push to vaccinate the world for past and present pandemics (real or hyped) resulted in countless unnecessary deaths. Again, I would advise reading Kennedy's book that details the fraud, cover-up, abuse of power, and pure evil on the part of the Fauci/Gates mafia. I will, however, reveal factual evidence of the serious side effects and, more importantly, the unnecessary deaths that have occurred from the current and *only* option mandated by fascist Fauci to treat the China Virus. But first, a little background on Fauci.

In 2010 the Bill and Melinda Gates Foundation formed an international vaccine community and created a Global Vaccine

Action Plan. This plan was to deliver lifesaving vaccines to the most vulnerable populations in the poorest countries over the next decade, which they called the "Decade of Vaccines." One member of the Leadership Council was Dr. Anthony S. Fauci, Director of NIAID, part of the National Institutes of Health.

Let's look back on Fauci's career to see why a ruthless billionaire like Gates would team up with Fauci. In 1988, while he was director of the NIAID, Fauci also took on the role of Director of the Office of Aids Research. In 1989 Fauci announced that the NIH had been conducting a successful clinical trial for the drug Azidothymidine (AZT) to help treat AIDS. At that time, this drug had been approved faster than any previous drug in the history of the FDA and was the most expensive drug ever marketed. AZT was the only antiretroviral drug that had received FDA approval for treatment of AIDS since the epidemic began, and the decision to approve it was based on a single study that has long since been declared invalid.

AZT had actually been developed twenty-five years earlier as a chemotherapy drug to treat cancer. But its use for that was stopped due to the fact that it was so toxic, expensive, and ineffective in fighting cancer. Even worse, other drugs such as Bactrim that were presented to treat HIV were declined by Fauci. Does this sound familiar with current therapeutics that have proven effective to treat COVID-19 being shunned by Fauci and his corrupt cohorts. Despite flawed and abandoned clinical trials and knowledge that AZT could be more detrimental than good, Fauci pushed it worldwide anyway. As a chemotherapy type of drug, AZT destroys white blood cells and damages bone marrow, central nervous system, liver, muscle tissue, brain, and kidneys. Fauci's clinical trials for AZT included unthinkable testing on children. But that's not surprising since we have recently learned that Fauci has stooped so low to allow the abhorrent practice of abusing man's best friend in what is referred to as *Beagle Gate.*

In 1992, New York's child welfare department partnered with Fauci's NIAID to have minority and underprivileged children, who were living in foster care, become the lab rats for Fauci and his pharma buddies to test for HIV drugs. At least eighteen children died, and many others suffered other serious side effects. Many of these vulnerable children didn't even have HIV yet were given drugs anyway. There were investigations into this tragedy, but Fauci used his power and the threat of withholding money from hospitals and others to avoid showing accurate records. Somehow, Fauci and others eluded being held accountable for these despicable and illegal actions.

Kennedy's book presents numerous published research and investigative articles from whistleblowers that spell out the hideous actions of a *mad scientist* and his cronies to make vaccines for COVID-19 and other "pandemics." Kennedy reveals jaw-dropping details and repeated incidents where Fauci has caused harm through deceptive practices, became mega-wealthy from big pharma, and wielded his narcissistic power to avoid being held accountable—at least for now.

Besides his unscrupulousness with AIDS, Fauci was again front and center in his fraudulent involvement with other pandemics (most of which failed to "pan" out). Those were: the bird flu of 2005, the swine flu of 2009, and Zika in 2015. With all of these, he spewed out fear and panic-laced warnings, all for the purpose of forcing people to take his vaccine *du jour.* Yes, people were infected, and many died. Yet, the number of infections and deaths certainly didn't reach the pandemic levels about which he had emphatically warned. Regardless, Fauci still made a bundle of money each time. Keep in mind that the NIH is a co-owner of the Moderna patent, so they have a vested financial interest in keeping these vaccines going.

And, not surprising, pharmaceutical companies are exempt from litigation. In 1986 Congress passed the National Childhood Vaccine Injury Act (NCVIA), which protects vaccine manufacturers from liability. I wonder if this "Act" would pass muster and give immunity to big pharma if we are forced to take the jab against our will in order to retain our employment?

Speaking of money, how is it that this appointed federal bureaucrat is the highest-paid employee of all four million federal employees in the federal government, even more than the President of the United States. In 2019, Fauci's annual salary was increased to $417,608. Between 2010 and 2019, he made (not earned) $3.6 million in salary. His annual retirement, should we be blessed with him retiring ASAP, will be $350,000 annually. That's just a drop in the bucket compared to what he has received from big pharma—those glorious makers of vaccines.

Then the question comes up concerning if POTUS could fire Fauci. That would be difficult. Fauci falls into the category of a "Title 42" employee. That's a special federal employment category for scientists and specialized consultants who work mostly in the Health and Human Services Department or the Environmental Protection Agency. While they don't have normal civil service protections, they can only be fired through a specific process. However, POTUS could certainly remove him from the COVID-19 Task Force. Don't hold your breath. Remember who currently holds that position.

Before we move on to our current pandemic, let's disclose another truth. Most Americans are not "anti-vaxxers." Historically, many vaccines have proven to be worthwhile in treating certain diseases. Just as no vaccine is perfectly effective, no vaccine is perfectly safe. And it is evident that in one year since the COVID-19 "vaccines" have been administered, the number of adverse effects (including death) is of great concern. That, coupled with the lack of transparency, misinformation, cover-ups of factual information, and the numerous flip-flop statements uttered by almighty Fauci, has caused Americans to carefully consider if they *choose* to get the jab or not.

Furthermore, the COVID-19 vaccine is unique in many ways. Most vaccines are created from the actual virus they are designed to treat. But the COVID-19 vaccines are synthetic. DNA is found inside the cells of every living thing. It's protected in a part of the cell called the nucleus. The genes are the details in the DNA blueprint for all the physical characteristics that make each one of us unique.

The information from our genes has to get from the DNA in the nucleus out to the main part of the cell (the cytoplasm), where proteins are assembled. Cells rely on proteins to carry out the many processes necessary for the body to function. These proteins are carried out via messenger RNA, or mRNA for short. These genetic vaccines use genes to *create* antibodies, whereas traditional vaccines introduce a small amount of the virus that *causes* our natural antibodies to do their thing. The risk with mRNA vaccines is that it can cause the virus to create more disease in the body than would be if no vaccine had been given. So technically, the COVID-19 "vaccine" isn't truly a vaccine.

And what about children? Is COVID-19 rampantly infecting five to eleven-year-old children? Should this age group get the jab? On October 26, 2021, Dr. Eric Rubin, who is a member of the FDA's Vaccines and Related Biological Products Advisory Committee (VRBPAC), had an alarming response to a question posed to the committee. This panel was asked, "Based on the totality of scientific evidence available, do the benefits of the Pfizer-BioN-Tech COVID-19 vaccine when administered as a two-dose series outweigh its risks for use in children five to eleven years of age?" Dr. Rubin's response was, "We're never gonna learn about how safe the vaccine is until we start giving it; that's just the way it goes." And we've been told for over a year now to follow the science. Despite Fauci's claim, "I am science," he nor the FDA seem to be following that mantra. Dr. Rubin's response sounds eerily familiar to neurotic Nancy's quote, "We have to pass the bill, so we can find out what is in it" (regarding the Obama Care bill). One other tidbit; when vaccine makers submit their papers to the FDA for the Emergency Use Authorization (EUA), that is *not* the same as a full FDA approval.

On June 21, 2021, the World Health Organization (WHO) clarified which population groups should receive COVID-19 vaccines. The WHO's website stated, "Children should not be vaccinated for the moment. There is not yet enough evidence on the use of vaccines against COVID-19 in children to make recommendations for children to be vaccinated against COVID-19. Children and adolescents tend to have milder disease compared to adults." The FDA has not followed that recommendation, however, and has rolled out vaccines for children five to eighteen years old. That is amazing when you think that it has been less than a year since vaccines were given to children, which is a short time to gather safety data. We should never put anything into a child without a minimum of three to five years of research for safety. Many of the children that have suffered adverse effects and/or death were healthy prior to receiving the jab. Children are not lab rats but don't tell that to Fauci. The latest update is Pfizer is seeking a EUA for infants six months old!

The Vaccine Adverse Event Reporting System (VAERS) is the primary government-funded system for reporting adverse vaccine reactions for all vaccines. These reports are updated and released on a weekly basis. The following charts include data from the VAERS website pertaining to adverse effects (including deaths) from COVID-19 vaccines from December 14, 2020, to December 17, 2021. The third chart summarizes total deaths from COVID-19 for all ages.

VAERS Summary for COVID-19 Vaccines through 2/11/2022

All charts and tables below reflect the data release on 2/18/2022 from the VAERS website, which includes U.S. and foreign data, and is updated through: **2/11/2022**.

High-Level Summary	COVID19 vaccines (Dec'2020 - present)	All other vaccines 1990-present	US Data Only COVID19 vaccines (Dec'2020 - present)	US Data Only All other vaccines 1990-present
Number of Adverse Reactions	1,119,063	871,655	760,102	758,627
Number of Life-Threatening Events	27,305	14,385	11,912	9,933
Number of Hospitalizations	130,774	83,256	54,081	38,969
Number of Deaths	23,990*	9,547*	10,909	5,295
# of Permanent Disabilities after vaccination	43,476	20,853	12,569	12,890
Number of Office Visits	173,801	49,933	150,074	47,755
# of Emergency Room/Department Visits	119,353	212,689	94,383	203,145
# of Birth Defects after vaccination	926	194	470	106

*Note that the total number of deaths associated with the COVID-19 vaccines is more than double the number of deaths associated with all other vaccines combined since the year 1990.

Cumulative Reported Deaths After Vaccination - 1 Year Summary

Data obtained from CDC's VAERS

● Covid-19 ● All Other Vaccines ● Unknown

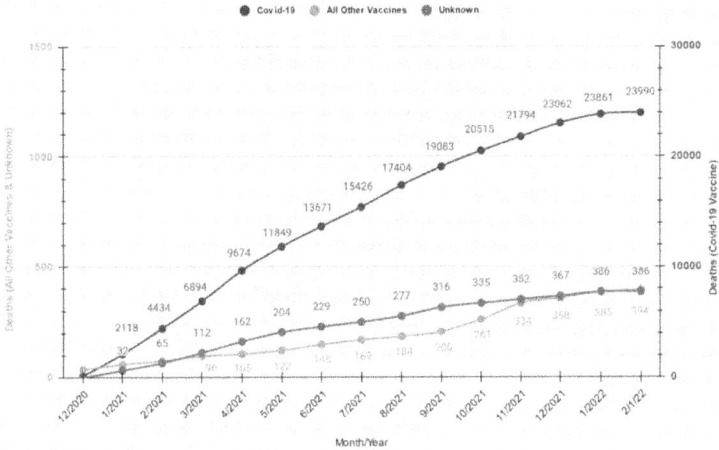

Month/Year

Reported Deaths by Year, COVID19 vs. All Other Vaccines, Cumulatively

Data Obtained from CDC's VAERS

● COVID19 Vaccines cumulative ● All Other Vaccines cumulative

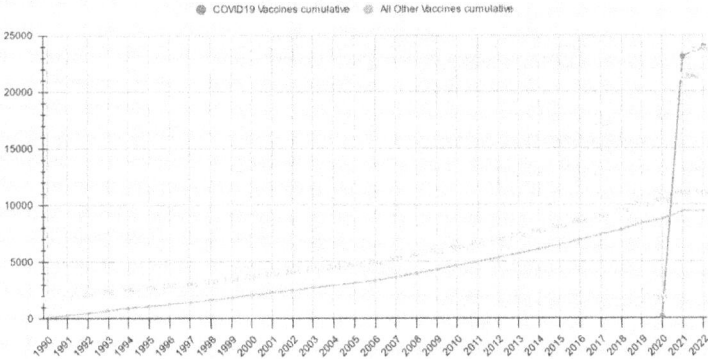

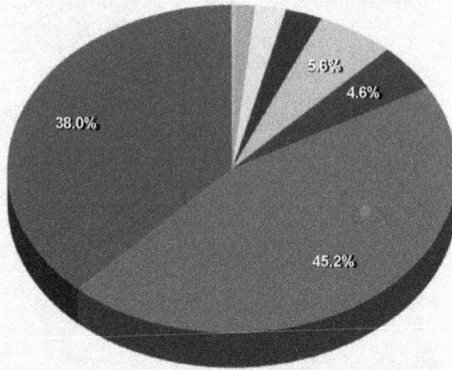

Age Distribution of Reported Deaths After COVID19 Vaccination

Data obtained from CDC's VAERS

5.6%

4.6%

38.0%

45.2%

● 0_17 ● 18_29 ● 30_39 ● 40_49 ● 50_59 ● 60_64 ● 65_ ● unknown

These are only four of the numerous charts and graphs from a government reporting agency that clearly show that the COVID-19 vaccines pose quite a risk. And yes, so does the disease itself, but mainly in people over the age of sixty-five; and those with co-morbidities such as obesity, diabetes, and chronic lung disease, to name a few. It should also be noted that this data might not be completely accurate based on the fact that doctors and hospitals don't always submit adverse reaction events. Furthermore, many of the reported deaths were reported as COVID-19 deaths, even if someone died *with* COVID-19 rather than *from* COVID-19. In other words, patients admitted to the hospital as a result of car accidents or heart attacks and who died from those causes may have tested positive for COVID-19. Because of merely testing positive, the cause of death was reported as COVID-19 rather than the actual cause of death. We're not downplaying the deaths that have taken place as a result of the China Virus; we just want truth and accuracy instead of adding to the fear.

Speaking of testing, it is alarming that the Biden administration dropped the ball on ordering the necessary number of tests when the Delta variant and the Omicron variant rolled into America. Wasn't it sleepy Joe who campaigned that he was going to "shut down the virus"? This has caused long, long lines for people to get tested. It's puzzling why people who have zero symptoms of anything wait in long lines to get tested (when the results of which would likely be negative) then possibly contract the disease on the subway going home. People who are certain they have been around someone recently infected with COVID-19 and/or those who are currently experiencing symptoms should be the only ones tested, especially since bumbling Biden didn't order enough tests.

Okay, on to the topic that makes ninety percent of Americans spitting mad (oops, shouldn't say spit when discussing this topic) — *masks*! If masks are so effective, then why on earth do fully vaccinated and boosted Americans, including those who have already had the China Virus, either get infected for the first time or have a breakthrough case?

After flip-flop, Fauci changed his original recommendation at the onset of the China Virus to not wear masks; he has been relentlessly hounding us ever since that we must wear masks — or else. Fauci sent an email on February 5, 2020, to former Obama Health and Human Services Secretary Sylvia Burwell that store-purchased masks do little to stop the spread of the disease. The email states, "The typical mask you buy in the drug store is not really effective in keeping out the virus, which is small enough to pass through the material. It might, however, provide some slight benefit in keeping out gross droplets if someone coughs or sneezes on you.

I do not recommend you wear a mask." He can't even follow his own advice. Since then, millions of Americans have been forced to believe that the only way they can protect themselves against this virus, besides getting vaccinated, is by strapping a piece of cloth around their noses and mouths. Mainstream and social media leftists and the current confused administration repeatedly scold, shame, and punish anyone who questions this unscientific guidance. There have been more studies on how ineffective masks are than studies on how effective they claim to be.

So if you still feel that masks are effective in stopping the spread of COVID-19 airborne droplets, try this little experiment. This was actually demonstrated in a video by viral immunologist Dr. Byram Bridle to prove that the very tiny aerosol droplets from COVID-19, as well as basic inhaling and exhaling aerosol droplets we do through simply breathing, can easily pass through the pore sizes of both surgical and cloth masks worn by millions. So, here we go. Get a pair of your glasses (sunglasses will work as well). Now, to clean the lenses, we typically breathe on them to form the aerosol mist on the lens. That makes it easy to clean with a soft cloth. However, this time, put on not one, not two, but three surgical masks on your face. Now, breathe on the lenses and see that you will still form the aerosol mist to clean the lens. Masks do not stop small droplets the size of COVID-19 droplets (which are smaller than droplets from our breath) from coming through the masks! Now that's following the science!

Why do you think fully vaxxed and boosted Americans are still mandated to wear them? It is not supported by science. Prior to 2020, multiple studies on the efficacy of mask-wearing (especially for healthcare workers) have been published by CDC, New England Journal of Medicine, Lancet, British Journal of Medicine,

Nature, JAMA, PubMed, and many other professional venues. Nearly all these studies, whether randomized control studies or clinical observational studies, found that mask-wearing to prevent transmission of infectious viruses were inconclusive at best and ineffective at worst. Experts universally agree that there's simply no replacement for thorough, frequent hand-washing for preventing disease transmission.

And look how most Americans wear these silly face rags, with noses exposed, mouths exposed, and some wear them like a beard. We sneeze and cough into them and constantly adjust them with our germy hands. How often do we change them out or wash our cloth masks? We are just plastering a pile of bacteria and germs onto our faces as we go about our day. Unbelievable! And our poor children, they have to suffer all day in a classroom, barely able to understand what the teacher is saying because her mask makes her sound like an airline pilot announcing, "We're about to land." And think about how important body language and facial expressions are in communicating. The human face is extremely expressive and able to convey countless emotions without saying a word. Facial expressions are universal. The facial expressions for happiness, sadness, anger, surprise, fear, and disappointment are the same across cultures. How is a three- or four-year-old supposed to read the non-verbal communication of their pre-school or kindergarten teacher, let alone his or her classmates, when they are hidden behind these ridiculous masks?

But a handful of narcissist billionaires, pseudo-scientists, and corrupt government officials are tenacious in using these tyrannical tactics and mandates as a means of control, power, financial gain, and pure evil. And now Americans are getting fed up, and rightfully so. Let's keep our foot on the pedal and continue to fight for our freedoms and stop this madness.

Okay, here's what really is the most alarming failure on the part of Fauci and his band of thugs. They have intentionally suppressed, ignored, and lied about the proven effectiveness of using *therapeutics* to treat the China Virus. Instead, TV doctor Fauci and his posse of mad scientists (who have not treated a single COVID-19 patient) are pushing vaccines and boosters despite their knowledge that therapeutics work. Fauci isn't supporting them because he doesn't make as much money off these as he does from big pharma's vaccine kickbacks. As he did with his AIDS treatment, where he denied the use of any other drug (except AZT), Fauci has obstructed the use of promising treatments to fight COVID-19, such as hydroxychloroquine, ivermectin, and monoclonal antibodies like Regeneron. Just think of the thousands and thousands of lives that would have been saved.

In his book *The Real Anthony Fauci*, Kennedy points to the lengths Fauci and Gates went to either destroy or prohibit doctors from prescribing Hydroxychloroquine (HCQ). One example in his book cites the following:

> A physician from Zambia reported to Dr. Harvey Risch that in some villages and cities, organized groups of buyers emptied drugstores of HCQ and then burned the medication in bonfires outside the towns. South Africa destroyed two tons of life-saving hydroxychloroquine in late 2020, supposedly due to violation of an import regulation. The US government in 2021 ordered the destruction of more than a thousand pounds of HCQ because it was improperly imported. 'The feds are insisting that all of it be destroyed and not be used to save

a single life anywhere in the world,' said a lawyer seeking to resist the senseless order.

This is absolutely shocking. Why did they do this in Zambia? Well, HCQ is a prescription drug that has been used since the 1940s. It was first used to treat malaria, which is prominent in African countries. In addition to being a malaria drug, today, HCQ is used to treat rheumatoid arthritis and lupus. You might find this interesting; as of January 3, 2022, Africa has reported 229,000 COVID-19 deaths compared to 828,879 in the United States. Gee, do you think there is a link to the fact that African citizens who have been taking HCQ for malaria (which is this same drug that has proven effective in treating COVID-19) have had fewer COVID-19 deaths than the US? But fascist Fauci wants to destroy this proven therapeutic and keep it from not only African citizens but American citizens as well — pure evil!

During one of his countless news conferences, Fauci emphatically responded "No!" when asked if HCQ might be used as a course of action to treat COVID-19. Fauci once again wielded his tyrannical power through threats and ordered pharmacists, doctors, and hospitals to cease prescribing HCQ to patients. In his book, Kennedy cites the following:

> In New York, Governor Andrew Cuomo drove up record death counts by ordering that physicians prescribe HCQ only for hospitalized patients. In Nevada, Governor Steven Sisolak prohibited both prescribing and dispensing chloroquine drugs for COVID-19. State medical licensing boards threatened to bring "unprofessional conduct" charges against non-complying doctors (a threat to their license) and to "sanction" doctors if they prescribed the drug. Most pharmacists were afraid to dispense HCQ, and on June 15, state pharmacy boards in Arizona, Ar-

kansas, Michigan, Minnesota, New Hampshire, New York, Oregon, and Rhode Island began refusing orders from physicians and retailers. Several hospitals commanded doctors to cease treating their patients with HCQ beginning June 15, 2020.

Let's see. Could it be that the hatred for Donald Trump, who enthusiastically endorsed the use of HCQ as a promising treatment for COVID-19, is the basis for the relentless dismissal of this proven drug? Yes, as well as his insatiable greed. The vaccine villain is certainly responsible for causing thousands of needless deaths by putting up roadblocks against affordable and effective treatments while bullying Americans to take vaccines whose efficacy is less than touted and poses dangerous adverse effects.

Fauci has led the same suppression campaign against the drug ivermectin, which won a Nobel Prize in 2015. Ivermectin is an FDA-approved drug for use in humans to treat a variety of parasitic infections. The antiviral activity of ivermectin has been shown against a wide range of RNA and DNA viruses, for example, dengue, Zika, yellow fever, and others. Versions of ivermectin are also used to deworm livestock, which has caused confusion and fueled political commentary about the use of the drug. Humans are not prescribed the versions that are for animals, so let's be clear on that.

One country that is singing the praises of ivermectin to treat COVID-19 is Japan. Japan is traditionally one of the more hesitant countries when it comes to trusting vaccine companies and even started their vaccine campaign for COVID-19 a couple of months after other countries. Despite the vaccines, Japan saw an increase in new infections in August 2021. The Japanese government was smart enough to look beyond vaccines to fight the pandemic. In September of 2021, they introduced ivermectin into their treatment protocol. The number of infections of COVID-19 cases decreased significantly, allowing citizens to avoid COVID booster jabs. Their government is claiming that ivermectin use is helping Japan permanently beat the pandemic, giving a crushing blow to big pharma, who unsuccessfully tried to suppress its use. Way to go, Japan!

And then, we have monoclonal antibody treatments, such as Regeneron. Monoclonal antibodies are lab-made proteins that can mimic the immune system's ability to fight off threats like COVID-19. When a patient is infected, it takes a little while for his or her body to produce antibodies that can help them fight the infection. These treatments, also known as mAbs, can speed up the body's ability to fight infection. The treatments are for people (vaccinated or not) infected with COVID-19 and for non-hospitalized adults and pediatric patients twelve years of age and older who have a risk of getting severe COVID-19. Monoclonal antibodies are meant to be used early in the course of the disease to keep it from progressing. A patient who is sick should get the treatment within ten days of experiencing symptoms. The mAbs have to be given by an infusion or, if getting an infusion would cause a delay in treatment, the Regeneron treatment can also be given by four subcutaneous injections.

The use of monoclonal antibodies for the treatment of COVID-19 gained national and international attention in October of 2020 when former President Trump received an antibody cocktail made by Regeneron after he was diagnosed with the illness. Shortly thereafter, two monoclonal compounds received Emergency Use Authorization (EUA) by the US FDA and were expected to be a key part of the response to the pandemic. But Fauci refused to promote this treatment option. When COVID-19 first hit us, and the country was shut down, a common protocol for infected people was that they were told to stay home and not return to the hospital unless their symptoms got worse, such as severe breathing problems. By then, it was too late for many. They were placed on ventilators and died. That certainly isn't a typical way doctors treat patients, is it?

So if therapeutics, like the ones previously illustrated, can subdue symptoms and prevent someone from experiencing serious illness when given early, why not use these treatments early and avoid the need to be admitted to a hospital?

Well, our vaccine villain finally came to his senses in this regard. In August 2021, Fauci said that people sick with COVID-19 could reduce their risk of hospitalization and death by as much as 85 percent if they receive monoclonal antibody treatments in the early stages of their illness. Well, hallelujah!!! I guess Florida Governor Ron DeSantis was right all along, as he had already set up several mAbs treatment facilities in Florida. But, hold on. Since then, Fauci put the brakes on either the manufacturing and/or distribution of these effective antibody treatments. He's evil!

Perhaps it's useless to recount the devastating effects that state-enforced lockdowns caused for our nation, but we should never forget. These policy implementations, with no precedent throughout American history, impacted every aspect of life in America. As expected, these lockdowns were needlessly extended in blue states. Did they work? Did they help shut down the virus? Not only did they fail to crush the virus, but they also did more damage than the virus itself. The list of collateral damages is long and tragic. It includes: increased suicide and attempted suicide deaths (especially among teens), increased health issues for lack of getting routine screenings and/or treatments for existing conditions, unemployment at all levels, small business closure, and increased drug overdoses.

Additional negative effects of lockdowns and mandates included more than a year of having our children receive the proper and essential education through in-person learning, socialization skills being hampered in toddlers, children, teens, and adults, increase in depression and other mental health disorders, an increase in obesity, which is one of the comorbidities to getting COVID-19 and other diseases and being prohibited from public worshipping of our Creator.

Then you have the absolute absurd mandates of threatening our first responders (fire, police, EMTs), hospital workers (including doctors and nurses who have been treating COVID-19 patients since the onset of the virus), and our military personnel with their jobs/careers unless they get the jab. How senseless is this? This mandate would actually put Americans at risk in terms of not only public safety and a lack of medical treatment but national security. Didn't the bad doctor (Fauci) take the Hippocratic Oath to do no harm? Perhaps not. The irony of this constant bullying by Fauci and others to get the jab was that in late December 2021 and into January 2022, more vaccinated people were infected with the China Virus than were the unvaccinated? Uhm, isn't that interesting? The good news is that America is starting to wake up because we are fed up with being lied to and forced to do things again our will. There are going to be some positive changes made in 2022, but we have to pray about them.

So, back to my earlier question: should there be only one (non-elected) bureaucrat dictating how we should fight this pandemic? I think you know the answer. Well, it could be God's providence at work here, but several websites, news publications, independent media sources, and journals have reported similar headlines, such as: "Gates, Fauci, and Daszak charged with Genocide in Court Filing" and "Bill Gates and Fauci Accused of 'Crimes Against Humanity' in International Criminal Court Complaint." This complaint was filed in the United Kingdom with the Prosecutor of the International Criminal Court on December 6th, 2021, by a team from the United Kingdom on behalf of the people. They are alleging crimes committed by UK government officials and international world leaders of various violations of the Nuremberg Code, crimes against humanity, war crimes, and crimes of aggression perpetrated against the peoples of the United Kingdom. Look it up for yourself.

It's a stunning forty-six-page legal filing that outlines numerous concerns about ethics violations, informed consent issues, inflating or manipulation of data, ignoring alternative treatment, the adverse effects of vaccines, and dangerous testing of vaccines. Here is a link to the legal document: https://www.docdroid.com/WUjv6iw/icc-complaint-7-1-pdf.

Oddly, however, is that as of February 2022, only a handful of online news outlets in the United States have reported this—and certainly not the mainstream media. So, not sure where this will lead. Yet as with everything else, it is in God's hands.

"Truthful words stand the test of time, but lies are soon exposed. Deceit fills hearts that are plotting evil; joy fills hearts that are planning peace!" (Proverbs 12:19–20, NLT).

Here's the bottom line. We don't trust the vaccine villain, the CDC, the FDA, the mainstream media, or the Biden administration concerning COVID-19. And, *we the people* certainly don't like bureaucrats like Fauci or the government issuing mandate after mandate.

If these mandates worked, why are we still having thousands of COVID-19 infections in 2022? And sadly, the vaccine villain has yet to be held accountable for all his wrong-doings: Fauci lied to Congress about the gain of function research to the Wuhan lab; up until late in 2021, he had blocked efforts to promote and utilize therapeutics that could have saved thousands of lives, he has flip-flopped his stance on masks, caused business (especially restaurants) to suffer economically, and he is doing his best to enforce vaccine passports for every American just to live their lives.

Speaking of vaccine passports, Fauci and his brood of vipers want to make us show our vaccine ID to simply eat in a restaurant (remember, COVID-19 won't get you when you are seated, just when you are standing or walking in the restaurant), but the left doesn't want voters to have to show an ID when they vote?

In late December of 2021, the vaccine villain reduced the quarantine time from ten days to five days because he saw the negative impact on the economy. Really? Do you mean he didn't see the negative impact for the past two-plus years? And now he thinks he's the economy czar for our country? Unfortunately, another group that has just about as much power as almighty Fauci is the Teachers Union. Talk about setting our country up to fail. Denying real in-person learning for students for one year is bad enough. But this corrupt leftist union wants to again resort to distance learning in 2022, particularly in Chicago, where there are more deaths of children due to shootings, than due to the China Virus. So, suck it up, teachers, and get back into the classroom.

So, Mr. Science, *we the people* want to exercise our freedoms to choose whether or not to get this particular jab for ourselves and/or for our children. We live in America, not a communist country, at least for now anyway. This whole pandemic (or pseudo pandemic) has imprisoned Americans in fear. A dear friend coined the phrase, "Know Fear=No Freedom!" Dr. (and I use that title loosely) Fauci, we are done with you and your constant fear-mongering. We are done with your mandates! M.A.N.D.A.T.E.=Making Americans Nauseous About Tyrannical Edicts!

God's Truth about Choice, Health, and Evil

The Book of Genesis in the Bible tells the story of the beginning of mankind. After God created Adam, He then planted a garden in Eden.

> Then the LORD God formed the man from the dust of the ground. He breathed the breath of life into the man's nostrils, and the man became a living person. Then the LORD God planted a garden in Eden in the east, and there he placed the man he had made. The LORD God made all sorts of trees grow up from the ground—trees that were beautiful and that produced delicious fruit. In the middle of the garden he placed the tree of life and the tree of the knowledge of good and evil.
>
> Genesis 2:7-9 (NLT)

God created human beings to have a right relationship with Him, to bring Him glory, to get to know and love Him, and be loved by Him. Initially, life in the garden was without sin. If God had not given Adam and Eve the choice, they would have essentially been robots simply doing what they were programmed to do.

"You may freely eat the fruit of every tree in the garden—except the tree of the knowledge of good and evil. If you eat its fruit, you are sure to die" (Genesis 2:15-17, NLT).

God created Adam and Eve to be "free" beings, able to make decisions and able to choose between good and evil. In order for Adam and Eve to truly be free, they had to have a choice. God gave us the choice to be obedient or not, and He spelled out the consequences.

Modern medical science has discovered many principles of good health, but they originated with God, Who designed and created the miracle that is the human body. Taking care of health is biblical and important, for God created us as body, soul, and spirit. We must not ignore the body's health and instead make choices that support good health, such as building and maintaining our natural immune system through good nutrition, supplements like vitamin C, zinc, vitamin D, and quercetin, getting adequate sleep, exercising, losing excess weight, and growing spiritually in our faith in God.

"Do not be wise in your own eyes; fear the Lord and shun evil. This will bring health to your body and nourishment to your bones" (Proverbs 3:7–8, NIV).

As mentioned in my previous book, *Our Crumbling Foundation – Will God Cancel Us?* we have ignored and/or removed God from most, if not all, aspects of our lives. It's obvious that has not been a wise choice. This chapter has revealed the truths, the lies, and the consequences of how this COVID-19 pandemic has been and could have been handled. So let's not succumb to the fear tactics being expelled by Fauci, the media, and the current administration about this virus. Again, it certainly wouldn't hurt to prayerfully lean on God when making your choices.

"Where God's love is, there is no fear, because God's perfect love drives out fear."
(1 John 4:18, NCV)

CHAPTER FOUR
— — —§— — —

No Accountability for Lawlessness —
Beginning at the Border

German philosopher Friedrich Nietzsche wrote, "Our crime against criminals lies in the fact that we treat them like rascals." Ain't that the truth! America, as well as the rest of the world, has always had crime. The US Constitution sets the framework for the US government, deals with core relationships within our society, and defines the rights of individuals. Criminal law is also foundational law in America. A District Attorney (DA) is a public official who is appointed or elected to represent criminal judicial proceedings in a particular district or county. A United States Attorney has the same responsibility at the federal level. They are all responsible for upholding the Constitution and enforcing the rule of law. The same oath of responsibility lies with Attorneys General at the state and federal levels.

So, it all depends on the color of your city, county, or state if your DA will keep their oath. If you live in a "red" jurisdiction, your odds are greater for the rule of law to be upheld and that criminals will be held accountable. On the other hand, if your color is "blue," odds are that your DA was funded by the evil George Soros, who hates America and wants lawlessness to reign. But, before we get into the weeds with the ugly facts of how Soros-backed jurisdictions are completely out of control, let's take a trip to our southern border.

Illegal immigration has been occurring for a long, long time. But 2021 was a stampede. Gee, I wonder what might have caused that. For starters, it's our open borders! Then-candidate Biden stated in the first Democratic primary debate that illegal immigrants should "immediately surge the border." And in another Democratic primary debate, Uncle Joe was asked if illegal aliens arrested by local police should be turned over to immigration officials, and he replied, "No." Hang on, it gets worse. In an interview with NPR in August 2020, Biden said illegal aliens should have access to the same benefits "everybody else has access to." The following month, Biden promised amnesty to all illegals. He didn't mention what he will do for citizens and legal immigrants—he cares more about the illegals than he does the rest of America.

The fiscal year 2021 was a historic record-breaking year for illegal alien apprehensions (or encounters as the Customs and Border Patrol (CBP) calls them). There were 1.72 million encounters at the southern border. Tragically, that doesn't count the thousands and thousands of illegal aliens who weren't stopped or caught crossing our border. Shortly after Biden's inauguration, migrants at the southern border were wearing professionally produced Joe Biden T-shirts that read, "Biden Please Let Us In!" Who knows who supplied those T-shirts; perhaps they just fell out of the sky. But, as the surge of illegal migration continued, our trusted Department of Homeland Security (DHS) Secretary Alejandro Mayorkas, as well as the Biden administration, refused to call the situation at the border a "crisis." They call it an "irregular migration influx event." The real crisis is that we have a few more years of this administration. Come quickly, 2024!

The apprehensions of illegal aliens with criminal backgrounds were quite frequent at the southern border. Border Patrol agents arrested 10,723 criminal aliens. Here's the breakdown:

	FY16	FY17	FY18	FY19	FY20	FY21	FY22
U.S. Border Patrol Criminal Non-citizen Arrests	12,842	8,531	6,698	4,269	2,438	10,763	3,662

Fiscal Year 2022 runs October 01, 2021 - September 30, 2022

Total Criminal Convictions by Type

This table organizes nation-wide convictions of criminal non-citizens by type of criminal conduct. Because some criminal non-citizens may be convicted of multiple criminal offenses, total convictions listed below exceed the total arrests noted in the above table.

	FY16	FY17	FY18	FY19	FY20	FY21	FY22
Assault, battery, domestic violence	1,007	692	524	299	208	1,178	74
Burglary, robbery, larceny, theft, fraud	825	595	347	184	143	825	134
Driving under the influence	2,458	1,596	1,113	614	364	1,629	194
Homocide, manslaughter	8	3	3	2	3	60	12
Illegal drug possession, trafficking	1,797	1,249	871	449	386	2,138	323
Illegal entry, re-entry	7,060	4,502	3,920	2,663	1,261	6,160	944
Illegal weapons possession, transport, trafficking	237	173	106	66	49	336	52
Sexual offenses	155	137	80	58	156	488	64
Other	2,544	1,851	1,364	814	580	2,691	439

Fiscal Year 2022 runs October 01, 2021 - September 30, 2022.
"Other" includes any conviction not included in the categories above.

A question comes to mind when looking at the chart where it shows that 6,160 arrests were made in fiscal 2021 for "illegal entry." It seems to me that all 1.72 million were illegal entries. Yet, the immigration laws are somewhat confusing; at least to me, they are. The US Code is a collection of laws passed by Congress. The Code of Federal Regulations (CFR) is a collection of regulations adopted by federal agencies. Regulations are valid only if authorized by law. Are you confused yet? The reason to explain this code stuff is to point out the US Code having to do with immigration.

Here's the first code regarding illegal entry into the United States: 8 US Code 1325, which basically states,

> Improper entry occurs when an individual enters, or even attempts to enter, the US at *a time or place that isn't designated by immigration officers*, avoids being inspected by immigration officers, or uses willfully untrue or misleading information in order to enter the US under false pretenses. This means that attempting to cross the border at any place other than a border inspection point or other official port of entry is illegal. Using fake entry documents or providing false information in order to unlawfully obtain entry documents may also be charged as illegal entry. [italics added]

Here's the second US Code to examine: 8 US Code 1158 regarding asylum, which states:

> Any alien who is physically present in the United States or who arrives in the United States *whether or not at a designated port of arrival* and including an alien who is brought to the United States after having been interdicted in international or United States waters, irrespective of such alien's status, may apply for asylum in accordance with this section or, where applicable. [italics added]

So, it's considered illegal entry if an alien crosses or attempts to cross the border unless it is at a designated port of entry. But that's what is happening. Illegal aliens are crossing all along the southwestern border (and even Florida, now that I think of it). Ah, but you *can* cross the border anywhere just as long as you say the magic word "asylum," and technically, that is not considered illegal entry. Why don't they change the law, code, rule, or whatever you want to call it to make the only place an immigrant can enter the US and claim asylum is at a designated port of entry. Also, make it mandatory that they remain in Mexico until immigration officials can evaluate the credibility of the asylum claim. Okay, I got side-tracked a bit, so back to the impact, this "illegal" immigration is having on all of us. It even impacts people who have entered the US legally, especially those who spent nearly two years after filing to become a US citizen. God bless those who do things the legal way.

Mexico is an asylum-granting country, and those third-country nationals who claim that they are fleeing harm in their own country can always claim asylum in Mexico. The fact that they haven't raises the question of whether it is fear of harm at home, or opportunity in the United States, that has brought them to this point. We must change our Asylum Law — immediately!

Illegal aliens have come from countries all over the world to cross our borders. They have subsequently been distributed all over our country by plane, train, or automobile whether CBP released them or they were one of the "got-aways." Some were temporarily housed in government camps and/or hotels (at taxpayers' expense), while others had clandestine flights and then dumped in mainly "red" states in the middle of the night (that's right, Jen Psaki, it was the middle of the night). So, where are these millions of illegal aliens sleeping now? Are they working? What about their children (if they are their actual children)? Are they enrolled in school? Do they have money for food? How many of them have required medical care (emergency or not)? Do they have transportation? How many of them don't speak English? You might be surprised to know that the United States has no official language. So, who knows, we may someday all be speaking Spanish or some other language from where the majority of illegal aliens may come.

It's a strong possibility that the answer to these questions is government handouts. While federal benefits are supposed to be off-limits, in practice, many are not. More than 25,000 undocumented workers receive subsidized housing, according to the US Department of Housing and Urban Development. Children receive free education, and most qualify for English lessons and free school breakfast and lunch. Educational cost estimates are understated because they do not include, for example, the costs of Limited English Proficiency (LEP) instruction or the costs of remedial instruction to students with educational gaps.

In addition to the millions of illegal aliens entering our country at our southern border, thousands of Afghan refugees (most of whom were not thoroughly vetted) have been resettled across America as a result of the deplorable way we militarily withdrew from Afghanistan in August 2021. So think about how a school teacher (provided they're not in the Chicago school districts refusing to go to work) can maintain any semblance of order in the classroom with non-English speaking children from Latin America, Afghanistan, Haiti, Zimbabwe, Yemen, China, and countless other nations. Children who possess vastly different educational experiences and/or different cultural backgrounds create a recipe for chaos and limited learning to take place. These migrants are flooding our already overcrowded classrooms for free education on the American taxpayers' dime.

And what about the environmental costs? Environmentalists and the "green new dealers" are turning a blind eye to the impact those crossings have on the areas through which they are trampling. It is estimated that each illegal alien leaves, on average, six to eight pounds of trash during their journey across the desert. Besides human waste, most of the other trash is not biodegradable. But it's all okay because Uncle Joe told them to come. We ought to send AOC and her posse to these border states to clean up the trash!

Biden supporters on the left like to portray all of the illegal aliens now flooding across the southern border as benign individuals simply seeking a better life. For many, that's true. Unfortunately, too many illegal aliens have already chosen a life of crime and want to cash in, so to speak, on those unlawful activities once they arrive in the United States. Most of this batch of illegals are the ones that snuck by Border Patrol agents. But, not to worry — as Friedrich Nietzsche said, they are just "rascals."

In the last two years, ICE (Immigration and Customs Enforcement) officers made 266,000 arrests of aliens with criminal records, including those charged or convicted of 100,000 assaults, 30,000 sex crimes, and 4,000 violent killings. Now, remember, ICE is mainly responsible for immigration enforcement in the interior of the country, while CBP is responsible for enforcement at the border. So that is in addition to the 10,763-plus arrests of aliens with criminal backgrounds that the CBP performed at the border in fiscal 2021. To make matters worse, liberal states, counties, and cities have developed policies declaring to be "sanctuary" jurisdictions. State legislatures can pass a law forbidding state officials from enacting sanctuary policies in their states, but the blue states don't.

Furthermore, state officials who are concerned about local jurisdictions implementing so-called "sanctuary" policies that prevent local sheriffs, police officers, and other law enforcement officials from communicating with federal officials over the immigration status of aliens who have been arrested for committing local crimes should be aware of a federal law that bans such a policy. The Illegal Immigration Reform and Immigrant Responsibility Act of 1996 states the following:

> Sec. 642 [A] Federal, State, or local government entity or official may not prohibit, or in any way restrict, any government entity or official from sending to, or receiving from, the Immigration and Naturalization Service information regarding the citizenship or immigration status, lawful or unlawful, of any individual.

When the first sanctuary cities began to form in the 1980s, the idea of police cooperation on the federal and state level to enforce immigration policy did not exist. It would not be until 1996 that this federal law was enacted to ensure the total cooperation between state, local, and federal agencies. This legislation requires authorities to share information regarding criminal illegal aliens in custody with federal immigration authorities without exception. Failing to do so creates another layer of disrespect for the law. Here's a typical scenario: first, the illegal alien breaks the law by stepping foot on American soil illegally. Then the illegal alien flees to a sanctuary city. Next, the illegal alien rapes and murders someone and is caught and arrested. Finally, the sanctuary jurisdiction which the illegal alien chose in the first place violates federal law when they fail to notify immigration authorities. But not to worry, this same jurisdiction happens to have a "no bail" policy. So, they are released. The illegal alien has more rights than his victim. When one law is left unenforced, then all sorts of other laws are weakened.

It is unthinkable that the Biden administration, and his completely inept vice president, cackling Kamala, and his clueless HHS Secretary, mindless Mayorkas, must hate our country so much that they would allow this lawlessness to continue at the border. Do they really want more and more Americans to die due to the pipeline of enormous quantities of illegal drugs that pour across our borders? Biden can shut the Keystone Pipeline, which benefits America, but do nothing to stop the fentanyl, heroin, meth, and cocaine pipeline that kills thousands of Americans.

It was tragic enough that China gave us the COVID-19 pandemic, but China is a major source of another plague that has and continues to kill thousands of Americans each year — Fentanyl. CBP reported confiscating 11,201 pounds of fentanyl and 624,500 total pounds of drugs between October 1, 2020, and September 30, 2021. In the previous fiscal year, CBP seized 4,791 pounds of the drug.

This doesn't count the "got-aways" who have smuggled in thousands of pounds of lethal drugs that have ended up in every state. There has reportedly been enough fentanyl confiscated in the past year to kill every man, woman, and child in the United States. Drug overdose deaths in America have now exceeded a hundred thousand deaths annually.

Now, these drugs don't cross the border on their own. Human smugglers or "coyotes" charge up to $60 thousand per alien, oftentimes bringing them on long journeys through the Mexican desert. There's a difference between human smuggling and human trafficking. A human smuggler, like a coyote, helps people get across the border for a fee and then generally lets them go. It's kind of what the Biden administration is doing with "smuggling" people to red states in the dark of night; only this time, it's for free. Human traffickers, on the other hand, exploit their victims—essentially selling them as slaves. Many migrants turn to coyotes because they are denied refugee status, or they don't take the time to apply for refugee status because they fear for their lives. In other cases, people are unfamiliar with the visa application process or are unwilling to wait for the process.

Numerous immigrants die trying to cross the desert each year, and while some are found (providing closure for their families), others are simply never heard from again. Immigrants have also died while trapped in trucks and shipping containers; some have drowned while trying to cross the Rio Grande, while others have been shot by members of Mexican cartel gangs.

With more than sixteen thousand frontline CBP officers and Border Patrol agents protecting over nineteen hundred miles of land at the US/Mexico border, it is still a daunting task to contain or manage illegal entry across our southern border. Whether through forced labor, drug and sex trafficking, or other criminal offenses, these atrocities are increasing with Biden's open-border policy. And let's not forget that his avoidable surge of illegal aliens occurred during the COVID-19 pandemic. Think how many infected people pouring into our country added to the spread of the China Virus. It's also amazing how these illegals aren't subject to mask mandates or vaccine mandates. How is that? Neither Uncle Joe, cackling Kamala, mindless Mayorkas, nor the far-left media will even speak a word of this dangerous hypocrisy.

Could the number of arrests of illegal aliens with criminal records be reduced? Could the number of "got-aways" be reduced? Could the number of deadly drugs entering our country be reduced? Could the number of aliens being illegally trafficked into our country be reduced? Could we have had fewer victims from criminal activity on the part of illegal aliens once released into our country? Could we have less spread of the China Virus if illegals weren't allowed to freely roam our nation? And, could we have fewer illegal immigrants even make an attempt to come to our southern border in the first place. The answer is yes. It's called a wall!

On his very first day in office, President Joe Biden made it clear he is ideologically opposed to building walls. He has stated that he doesn't like them, they're unfriendly, and they don't work. That's why he halted construction on the wall along the Mexican border. But let's look back a few years and see what Uncle Joe said during a speech to a South Carolina Rotary Club in November 2006. Biden said,

> I voted for 700 miles of fence. And the reason why I, parenthetically, why I believe the fence is needed does not have anything to do with immigration, as much as drugs. I'm the guy that wrote the national crime bill. I'm the guy that wrote the national drug trafficking. I'm the guy that wrote the law that set up a drug czar. And let me tell you something, folks, people are driving across that border with tons, tons — hear me — tons of everything from byproducts for methamphetamine to cocaine to heroin.

On January 20, 2021, Biden's first day in office, he signed an executive proclamation, which states in part:

> Like every nation, the United States has a right and a duty to secure its borders and protect its people against threats. But

building a massive wall that spans the entire southern border is not a serious policy solution. It is a waste of money that diverts attention from genuine threats to our homeland security. My administration is committed to ensuring that the United States has a comprehensive and humane immigration system that operates consistently with our Nation's values. In furtherance of that commitment, I have determined that the declaration of a national emergency at our southern border in Proclamation 9844 of February 15, 2019…was unwarranted.

The Trump administration had allocated approximately $16.4 billion to the border wall construction and related projects. Of that, $10 billion was allocated to the Department of Defense (DOD) for the actual border wall construction. These funds were designated to construct 338 miles of new primary and secondary walls where no barriers had previously existed. Additionally, 400 miles had been funded to repair damaged and/or inadequate existing primary and secondary walls. When Trump left office, 453 miles of total primary and secondary walls had been completed. So, let's do the math. That means that 285 miles along our southern border remain unprotected by a border wall. But Biden wants to protect the border of Ukraine!

This was a very costly executive (dis)order on the part of ole Joe. In July of 2021, the Senate Subcommittee on Government Operations and Border Management issued a scathing report which outlined the fact that halting construction on the border wall had cost taxpayers nearly $2 billion dollars since Joe's pen was so busy on January 20, 2021. Additionally, the Biden administration is still paying contractors at least $3 million per day to simply keep watch on the steel and other fencing materials as it deteriorates in the desert sun. That's like the Biden administration paying qualified workers more unemployment to sit home rather than go back to the numerous jobs that are available. Again, no accountability for wasting our money, weakening our national security, adding to COVID-19 infections, increasing crime, or negatively impacting our schools and economy—all because he hates Trump. Come on, Brandon!

No wonder the countless number of illegal aliens enter our country without having an encounter with a border patrol agent. These agents are overwhelmed with a daily average of three thousand illegals, for whom they have to take to a facility for processing, which includes a health screening and criminal background check. Many illegals cross in large groups in certain areas along the un-walled border. It doesn't take "Wiley Coyote" long to figure out that while the "Road Runner" border patrol agents are busy with asylum claimers, that leaves miles of un-bordered areas in which to cross undetected into the US. Now, don't you think if the wall had been completed, it would greatly reduce the places where undetected illegals could cross? It might even deter illegals from making the trip in the first place to try to come to America. It isn't rocket science.

Besides flip-flopping from his stance on border walls from 2006, the hypocrisy doesn't stop here. Now, Uncle Joe feels walls make things more secure. Not at the southern border but on his private property at his Delaware beach house. In September 2021, the DHS awarded a contract to the tune of $456,548 to build a wall around Joe's home. And don't forget—it's taxpayer-funded. Just like neurotic Nancy felt she needed a wall around her workplace following the January 6 non-insurrection, Joe needs a wall around his home—probably so he doesn't wander off and get lost.

God's Truth about Immigration and Walls

The United States actually has a compassionate immigration policy for those who want to enter our country lawfully. However, that is not the question at hand. The question at hand concerns illegal immigration—whether it is wrong to violate a nation's borders and transgress its immigration laws.

> Do not take advantage of foreigners who live among you in your land. Treat them like native-born Israelites, and love them as you love yourself. Remember that you were once foreigners living in the land of Egypt. I am the LORD your God.
>
> Leviticus 19:33–34 (NLT)

In the Old Testament days, God gave the Israelites the Promised Land to be a sovereign nation that worshipped only one God. If a non-Jewish foreigner chose to live among the Jews, be obedient in learning about the God of Israel, and worship Him exclusively, then they were to be welcomed and treated like a native-born Israelite—with some restrictions on land ownership, etc. This is how God wanted to treat those who came into the land *legally*. If they wanted to remain, these foreigners were expected to fully assimilate into the Hebrew religion and culture before being allowed to enjoy the blessings and responsibility of full citizenship.

If we fast-forward to present times, we also welcome immigrants who come here legally and would like them to assimilate into our culture, language, and rules. Additionally, they have the freedom of religion to practice the faith of their choice. Immigrants are welcomed here through legal entry.

Yet God does have some things to say about illegal immigration. Remember, entering our country, or any country illegally, is breaking the laws of that nation.

Everyone must submit to governing authorities. For all authority comes from God, and those in positions of authority have been placed there by God. So anyone who rebels against authority is rebelling against what God has instituted, and they will be punished. Consequently, whoever rebels against the authority is rebelling against what God has instituted, and those who do so will bring judgment on themselves.

Romans 13:1–2 (NIV)

The biblical view of illegal immigration is that if an alien enters the United States illegally, then he/she is breaking the law. Those seeking to emigrate to another country should always obey the immigration laws of that country. At the bottom line, God is in favor of legal immigration and is against illegal immigration.

Let's now tackle God's view on borders. The government has a unique duty (and moral duty) to God and to its citizens. According to chapter 13 of the Book of Romans, it is the government's duty to enact justice, enforce the law, and protect the citizen. Numerous countries in the world have a physical barrier or wall to control immigration, smuggling, and national security. So, what does God think about border walls?

"God Most High gave the nations their lands, dividing up the human race. He set up borders for the people and even numbered the Israelites" (Deuteronomy 32:8, NCV).

In the world of the Old Testament, people built walls around cities to protect themselves from thieves, murderers, and other criminals and from foreign invaders who would seek to destroy the city. Citizens would enter the city, but they had to do so through the designated gate, so that city officials would have some control over who was coming in and going out. Safe walls gave peace and security to those inside their perimeter.

"May there be peace within her walls and safety within her strong towers" (Psalm 122:7, NCV).

"Do whatever good you wish for Jerusalem. Rebuild the walls of Jerusalem" (Psalm 51:18, NCV).

After seventy years of exile in Babylon, the Jewish people were able to return to Jerusalem and Israel as a whole. Almost one hundred years after the exile ended, Nehemiah left Persia and went to Jerusalem after hearing that the Israelites in Jerusalem were in danger because they had no wall to protect them and their city. Despite the nay-sayers, Nehemiah rallied the people to rebuild the wall around Jerusalem in record time.

> So the wall was completed on the twenty-fifth of Elul, in fifty-two days. When all our enemies heard about this, all the surrounding nations were afraid and lost their self-confidence, because they realized that this work had been done with the help of our God.
>
> Nehemiah 6:15–16 (NIV)

God does advocate border walls. There is hope, and it's time to return to God and rebuild God's wall of protection around our nation. If we sincerely desire to rebuild our nation and protect our sovereignty, there is much to be learned from the lessons in the Book of Nehemiah and other parts of God's Word.

— — —§— — —

Well, we have covered lawlessness at our southern border, but what about the rest of America? It's hard to know where to begin. Despite the fact that the enormous influx of illegal aliens at the border opens our country up to being victims of drug smuggling, human trafficking, gang activity, and all sorts of crimes, much of our rapid surge in criminal activity in our nation is homegrown.

Crime has always been a problem in the US and around the world. Yet, violent crime has become a tsunami in several major cities in America since the protests stemming from the police killing of George Floyd in Minneapolis in May 2020. Violent protests spread to other cities, which resulted in billions of dollars of damages to businesses, government and civic buildings being burned, rampant looting, and even homicides. The main people responsible were Black Lives Matter (BLM) and Antifa groups. It should be noted that not only has evil George Soros funded radical left-wing District Attorneys in several jurisdictions, but he has also given millions and millions of dollars to the BLM and Antifa.

Following the Floyd incident, city's leaders decided to defund the police, embrace strongly anti-police rhetoric, and jump on the "re-imagine policing' efforts"' This also spread across America mainly—fueled by corporate media. As a result of reducing funds and the fact that police officers were relentlessly demonized, several of them opted to resign or take an early retirement from their careers in law enforcement. Then, to make matters worse, Soros-funded radical left-wing DAs decided to stop prosecuting many crimes and criminals. So how much incentive would you have as a police officer if you knew the thug you just arrested would never be held accountable? How's that "re-imagining" working out?

In most states across the country, when someone is arrested and charged with a crime, they are required to put down a refundable deposit to ensure that they will show up for their court date. If they don't have the cash available, they often turn to a commercial bond company that fronts the money on their behalf. If the person arrested cannot afford to pay their bail, they remain in jail until their court hearing. But this is not the case in some major radical left states such as California, New York, and Illinois. Let's see, don't these states also have those pesky Soros District Attorneys – Los Angeles DA, George Gascon, San Francisco DA, Chesa Boudin (whose parents were members of the "Weather Underground" and were convicted of murder in 1981), the newly-elected Manhattan DA, Alvin Bragg, and Chicago DA, Kim Foxx (who initially dropped the case against Jussie Smollett).

Let's see how things worked out in Chicago in 2021. Chicago is the nation's third-largest city and led the nation in homicides in 2021. Chicago's Medical Examiner reported 836 homicides in the city limits. Additionally, there were 4,000 victims of gunshot (both fatal and nonfatal). Records also show that the rogue bail reform policies resulted in 33 percent of those defendants released on the "get outta jail free" policy were soon thereafter charged with new violent crimes. And, let's be truthful – most of this violent crime is black-on-black crime. It truly is sad that more than half of all victims of homicide are black Americans. But even sadder is that most citizens who reside in these violent-torn communities are also black Americans who are victims as well. Don't these black lives matter?

The Biden administration and left-wing media have put their heads in the sand about all of this violent crime, that is, until recently. A "new" crime reared its ugly head and spread across America this year. It's called "smash and grab." It actually grew out of the protests in 2020, where the burning and looting of business were taking place during what CNN described as "peaceful protests." Instead of using matches to torch a building, the mobs now use sledgehammers (that they stole from Home Depot) to smash through store windows and display counters so they can loot to their heart's delight.

Since this new flash-mob crime wave is mainly targeting upscale businesses like Louis Vuitton and Nordstrom, the wealthy democrats (like Pelosi) are starting to take notice. Well, some Democrats are—but Alexandria Ocasio-Cortez (AOC) doesn't think it's a big deal. She was recently quoted to have said, "Allegations of organized retail theft are not actually panning out." What's not "panning out" is the denial, lies, and detrimental policies by these left-wing wackos. Hey AOC, are you denying that Los Angeles police have reported that there have been 7,542 smash-and-grab robberies from January to November 2021? This organized theft is estimated to cost retailers around $45 billion in losses in 2021. She even linked the expiration of the child tax credit to this rise in crime by stating, "And now people are stealing baby formula." I haven't seen much baby formula in Nordstrom or jewelry stores, have you?

So what do we do about it? Who votes these rogue district attorneys, mayors, governors, school board members, members of Congress, and presidents into office? And a more alarming question is, who re-elects them after the atrocities they display? Somehow we have to expose the truth to our liberal friends and family members, in a calm and convincing manner, to open their eyes to the fact that if we keep this kind of leadership going, America will no longer be America!

On January 27, 1838, Abraham Lincoln (before he became President of the United States) gave a speech to the Young Men's Lyceum. This speech was motivated by a recent tragic event that occurred a couple of months earlier, close to where Lincoln lived in Springfield, Illinois. A newspaper editor named Elijah Lovejoy was murdered by a pro-slavery mob. Lovejoy was a strong abolitionist and began an anti-slavery newspaper. Here is an excerpt from Lincoln's speech, which is so fitting and appropriate for us today:

But all this even, is not the full extent of the evil. By such examples, by instances of the perpetrators of such acts going unpunished, the lawless in spirit, are encouraged to become lawless in practice; and having been used to no restraint, but dread of punishment, they thus become, absolutely unrestrained. Having ever regarded government as their deadliest bane, they make a jubilee of the suspension of its operations; and pray for nothing so much, as its total annihilation. While, on the other hand, good men, men who love tranquility, who desire to abide by the laws and enjoy their benefits, who would gladly spill their blood in the defense of their country; seeing their property destroyed; their families insulted, and their lives endangered; their persons injured; and seeing nothing in prospect that forebodes a change for the better; become tired of, and disgusted with, a government that offers them no protection; and are not much averse to a change in which they imagine they have nothing to lose. Thus, then, by the operation of this mobocratic spirit, which all must admit, is now abroad in the land, the strongest bulwark of any government, and particularly of those constituted like ours, may effectually be broken down and destroyed—I mean the attachment of the People.

If you aren't moved by those words, you might want to put a mirror under your nose to see if you are still breathing. If our leaders and those in charge of enforcing the law and protecting our nation can't do their job, we need to vote them out of office immediately. If our Founding Fathers could see how far America has fallen away from our founding on Christian principles and the rule of law, they would be astounded. We should be astounded! We can't allow evil to multiply and take over our country. Let's get on our knees, seek His guidance, and forge ahead to reclaim our nation.

God's Truth about Lawlessness

Because we are all sinners living in a fallen world, crime will never be eliminated from this side of heaven. Yet, the leaders in government play a significant role in reducing crime and keeping the peace. But we need God's help in making that happen.

"Pray for rulers and for all who have authority so that we can have quiet and peaceful lives full of worship and respect for God" (1 Timothy 2:2, NCV).

Regardless of what society promotes, we must choose to live a life of integrity. We can make a difference in the world if we live a life based on moral absolutes and by letting honesty and integrity guide our decisions. Society changes as individuals change. We must lean on God through His Word and prayerfully seek His guidance in all things. Prayer is more powerful than anything else we can do for our nation. There is true power in prayer, and God knows it! We should not just rely on political power to make changes for us but, more importantly, rely on the power of God. He is always with us.

"The eyes of the LORD are in every place, keeping watch on those who are evil and those who are good" (Proverbs 15:3, NET).

"Remember, it is sin to know what you ought to do and then not do it" (James 4:17, NLT).

> "Doing what is right makes a nation great,
> but sin will bring disgrace to any people."
> (Proverbs 14:34, NCV)

CHAPTER FIVE

$-- -\S-- -$

Dumbing Down America —
Education of Hate, Hypocrisy, and Hysteria

Remember when the "3 Rs" (Reading, 'Riting, and 'Rithmatic) were the basics of educating our young children. Tragically, our education system today centers on the "3 Hs" — Hate, Hypocrisy, and Hysteria! We'll dive into this dreadful fact later. First, let's evaluate the reasons our schools are failing our students and America as a whole.

One primary cause of poor educational outcomes for students, which was more prevalent before COVID-19, is a serious lack of parental involvement. Learning, reinforcement, and parental interest is as vital outside the classroom as it is within the school. And this is not just a situation for people at lower socioeconomic levels. Many parents from middle and upper-class families fail to get involved in their children's education. With COVID-19, however, numerous parents were forced to get involved because schools were shut down and resorted to "remote learning." Despite all the negatives about that, there was a positive. Parents were finally exposed to what was really going on in the curriculums of their schools. It was transparency by accident.

Another reason our schools are failing is due to the overcrowded class sizes. It's tough on the students and tough on the teachers. Couple that with all the illegal alien children that are now steaming into our schools, many of whom do not speak English, and you have a recipe for disaster. Maybe that is why so many school districts are continuing to opt for COVID-19 caused distance learning, which is a huge failure in itself.

Prior to the China Virus, America's rankings in reading and math proficiency were pretty dismal. Although the US spends more money per student than any other country in the world, the educational system only ranks as the fourteenth best. The percentage of US residents who are literate (able to read and write) ranges between 65 and 85 percent. This wide range is due to a difference in how literacy is measured. Approximately 15 percent of the population can read at a university bachelor's degree level. Sadly, the majority of Americans are only able to read at a seventh or eighth-grade level.

One reason for low proficiency in reading and science is due to eliminating or altering phonics as a method of learning to read. Simply put, phonics is the relationship between letters and sounds. One of the best ways to describe phonics is as a code that breaks written language into comprehensible building blocks. If a child understands that a letter of the alphabet has a specific sound and that combinations of letters have corresponding specific sounds, then they can "decode" words as they read. Although phonics is considered to be an instructional reading method, it also helps children learn to write as well.

Sadly, the left-leaning educational establishment phased out the successful phonics method in the early 1990s and opted to go with their "sight-word" or "whole-word" approach to reading, which is basically memorizing words as a graphic shape or symbol. There are a ton of words to memorize simply by sight. Sight-reading may be faster at the beginning and look like fluency, but as the child expands into unfamiliar vocabulary later in their education, they aren't able to tackle new words easily—they stumble due to their weak and/or absent foundation in phonics.

Research shows that children who do not learn to read by the end of third grade are likely to remain poor readers for the rest of their lives. Additionally, they're likely to fall behind in other academic areas too. People who struggle with reading are more likely to drop out of high school, end up in the criminal justice system, and live in poverty. Educators often give the excuse that deficiency in reading is due to poverty. Well, how do you explain that one-third of America's struggling readers are from college-educated families?

Another failure to our educational system was the introduction of the "Common Core." Common Core (CC) came about in the Obama years and is basically a one-size-fits-all approach to learning. Common Core is the set of academic standards in mathematics and English language arts that define what a student should learn by the end of each school year in kindergarten through twelfth grade. In any case, national standards and tests change curriculum content, homogenize what is taught, and severely alter the structure of American K-12 public education. In fact, national standards don't actually help families or local schools improve their education—they only help number-crunching officials who distribute funding.

Common Core was initially adopted in some states as early as 2010, with Kentucky being the first state. Originally forty-six states passed laws adopting the Common Core standards in their schools. The four states that never adopted those standards were Virginia, Texas, Alaska, and Nebraska. Also, four states who have successfully withdrawn from the curriculum are Arizona,

Oklahoma, Indiana, and South Carolina. These eight states are typically Republican-controlled and are smart enough to reject Common Core.

Instead of respecting students' different levels of effort, ability, and individual strengths and interests, CC forces teachers to "teach to the test" and drill students with the same materials, so the entire class has at least a basic level of proficiency. Students who are high achievers in the classroom may not test well, and lower standardized test scores can affect their placement in classes, which may jeopardize their academic future. Also, teachers whose students perform well in the classroom but test poorly may see a negative impact on the teacher's evaluation and eventually their salary, and/or affect their seniority or placement, and could eventually even lead to termination.

Common Core was a massive change to American education and was rushed through without any real democratic process or empirical data supporting the value. Gee, doesn't that sound familiar? Can you say Fauci's villainess vaccines?

Some worry that corporate interests are the real force behind the CC since they'll reap huge profits from selling new tests and preparation materials. And wouldn't you know it? The Bill and Melinda Gates Foundation poured hundreds of millions of dollars into supporting the effort. First, they want to control the population and jab the planet with all sorts of vaccines; then, they also want to control education. Scary! So, no wonder Randi Weingarten and other elected officers to the American Federation of Teachers (AFT) and the radical leftist Education Secretary, Miguel Cordona, won't end Common Core — just follow the money.

Then these radical educators (which should instead be called propagandists) try to re-write history, distort the truth, question one's gender, and provoke more division and hate in our country. Look, history is history. We can't change or erase what has already taken place. We can't cancel it! Radical educators either speak and write about history with distorted mistruths, or they completely ignore history and the valuable lessons it provides. Why not tell all the facts — the good, bad, and ugly of our history as it really happened. The left also wants to topple statues of key figures of our American story and rename military bases named after Confederate leaders. Regardless of the fact that those choosing to participate in this senseless behavior probably don't really know much about our nation's history in the first place, they ignorantly see these symbols as something they need to destroy.

The author and poet Maya Angelou wrote, "History, despite its wrenching pain, cannot be unlived, but if faced with courage, need not be lived again." The great reverend, Dr. Martin Luther King Jr., was quoted: "We are not makers of history. We are made by history." The author's Pearl Buck take on history was, "If you want to understand today, you have to search yesterday." And sociology professor C. Wright Mills said, "Neither the life of an individual nor the history of a society can be understood without understanding both." Chew on these statements for a while — for they all make perfect sense.

Our history has several stains. But slavery is the one that stands out the most. Was it wrong? Yes! Did we realize it was wrong and correct the wrong? Yes, at least as a nation, we did. There will always be bad apples and extremists in every society who thrive on doing very bad things. Slavery has been in our world pretty much from the beginning of civilization.

Not to excuse America's involvement in slavery, but it is a little-known fact that slavery existed in Africa long before Europeans arrived in Africa for the purpose of capturing and/or purchasing Africans to take them to Europe and eventually having a trans-Atlantic route to America. Africans took other Africans as slaves as a result of personal disputes, for payment of debts, or from captured prisoners of war with a rival clan in Africa.

Sadly, it evolved to having some of these African slave owners selling slaves to Europeans who were in the slave trade business. Yet, many of these European slave traders hunted down and captured slaves and distributed them to other countries. Again, slavery is a horrible part of our nation's history and the history of other nations. It is wrong!

Our Founding Fathers owned numerous slaves, such as George Washington, Thomas Jefferson, James Madison, Benjamin Franklin, and Alexander Hamilton, to name a few. At some point in their lives, they all wished that slavery would be abolished. George Washington said that owning slaves was to him "the only unavoidable subject of regret." But are we going to erase all the accomplishments these great men achieved for our nation? Here's a newsflash—we are all sinners! We live in a fallen world. If we acknowledge our sins and change our ways and ask for forgiveness, we will be forgiven by the One Who counts. So the individuals and groups who are choosing to destroy symbols of our history, re-write history, and/or cancel our history are currently being sinful by doing so.

Besides discontinuing the educational method of phonics to teach reading, and incorporating the ineffective Common Core program, education officials (mostly with a liberal bend) phased out civics education in their curriculums. Or, they have given less emphasis to civics as a stand-alone subject and instead squeezed it into history classes. Most states have dedicated insufficient class time to understand the basic functions of government, the history of the Constitution and Bill of Rights, and American democracy. Recent surveys have shown that approximately only 25 percent of Americans can name all three branches of our US government. The Biden administration has their hair on fire to re-write voter laws because of what they falsely claim is "voter suppression." Well, it's highly likely that not having proper and adequate education in civics is also a form of voter suppression.

Our democratic system depends on citizens to take an active interest in the affairs of our government, understand how our government should act, and choose representatives who share their beliefs about the direction in which our country should go. When legislators know that their constituents do not know or care what they are doing, it gives them an incentive to cater to the lobbyists and special interest groups who *are* examining the legislators' actions. We don't need more lobbyists. We need informed and patriotic citizens and representatives.

It's pretty evident that communities whose citizens are civic-minded and civic-educated experience lower unemployment, lower crime, and stronger economies. Communities that lack knowledge of public affairs and the role of our government become victims of the corruption their elected representatives bring about because of the lack of interest and/or knowledge on the part of their constituents. It's another reason to get involved in your community's school board. Fight to bring back civics as a core subject in your school curricula. Our form of government is not a spectator sport. To maintain our freedom, we have the responsibility to be involved citizens.

Our radical leftists found a replacement for civics in our school—Critical Race Theory (CRT). This academic discipline (it's really just propaganda) was developed by Derrick Bell, a former Harvard Law professor in the 1970s and 1980s, and other scholars. It was founded on the premise that racism is a systemic issue that totally puts non-whites at a disadvantage. They contend that America was founded on white supremacy and oppression, and that remains at the core of our society today.

CRT expresses the old Marxist dichotomy of oppressor and oppressed. CRT proponents argue that all white people are inherently racist and that society should work to abolish the white race. They want to bring back radical segregation in all aspects of our society. And, of course, they are anti-capitalists.

But the real tragedy is that some schools are blatantly or covertly inserting CRT into their curricula. This dangerous propaganda teaches children that they are defined solely by their race and teaches children to hate each other and hate our country. Now isn't that delightful? CRT is totally counterintuitive. Teaching children to judge by race will only perpetuate racism.

Donald Trump said of CRT, "This is a Marxist doctrine holding that America is a wicked and racist nation, that even young children are complicit in oppression, and that our entire society must be radically transformed." If you don't like America, then leave—immediately! People with this type of agenda do not represent the majority of Americans. But they do wield lots of power and influence from the vast amounts of funding they get from evil individuals like Soros and Gates.

A main focus of the CRT movement is the "1619 Project." The 1619 Project attempts to amend the actual history of America. The central premise is that America was not founded in 1776 when the Constitution was ratified. According to this new interpretation, the functional founding of America occurred when the first enslaved Africans arrived on the North American continent.

Further, the author claims, the colonists fought the Revolutionary War primarily to protect the slave trade. They want to brand our founding documents – the Declaration of Independence and the Constitution – as immoral and thus unworthy of our allegiance. Slavery was not unique to the United States; it is a part of almost every nation's history, from Greek and Roman civilizations to contemporary forms of human trafficking. So what is the timeline of slavery in America? Most historians use 1619 as a starting point, when twenty Africans referred to as "servants" arrived in Jamestown, Virginia, on a Dutch ship. It's important to note, however, that they were not the first Africans on American soil. Africans first arrived in America in the late 16th century, not as slaves, but as explorers together with Spanish and Portuguese explorers. In 1619, people living in what is now America were living in colonies. The United States was *started* in slavery but *founded* in freedom in 1976. We formed a "more perfect union" but not a perfect union.

We are, and will always be, under construction. As great as America is, we have had some dark moments, particularly slavery segregation in the 18th and 19th-century America and Japanese internment camps during the Second World War. These events in our history drifted away from the motto proposed for the first Great Seal of the United States adopted by our Founding Fathers, *E Pluribus Unum*, which means "Out of Many, One." Yet, we strive to be a nation that is united. Erasing or altering the truth about our nation's history, as the 1619 Project and Critical Race Theory experiments do, only divides us and hampers our desire to learn from our past failures and overcome them. Let's educate our children with truth. God bless America!

But perhaps the most ludicrous stunt the NEA and the corrupt teachers' unions have implemented is the comprehensive LGBTQ+ (believe me, they have added a lot more letters so nobody is left out) agenda. This insane agenda includes indoctrination of children about transgender initiatives through curriculum and storybooks that plant seeds of gender confusion in children and push the deceptive idea that children can choose their gender. This is child abuse and is akin to the "grooming" that pedophiles effectuate on vulnerable children.

In tandem with Critical Race Theory, these gender studies are flooding America's kindergarten classrooms in radical ways. Drag queens are performing storytime for young children in libraries and some schools, where they read books about gender identity like *Sparkle Boy* and *Jacob's New Dress*. They're not simply reading stories to the children—their reading is enhanced with provocative and sensual gestures and innuendos, totally inappropriate for any school-age child. Many kindergarteners don't yet know how to tie their shoes, let alone read. Teachers should focus on these basics instead of promoting identity confusion that may never have become an issue in the child's existence.

What makes this whole scheme even more heinous is many school districts now have policies in place that not only allow but require teachers and administrators to withhold information from parents concerning gender identity issues of the student and/or the goings-on about this agenda on the part of school authorities. These policies to subvert parental rights to oversee the education and care of their children represent a deceptive overreach by our public schools and is a clear violation of the equal protection requirement of the Fourteenth Amendment. Additionally, it is a violation of the 1974 Family Educational Rights and Privacy Act, which grants parents the rights to their children's school records. There is a ton of effort on the part of teachers and school counselors to enable and promote extreme measures when they assess and/or assume a child might be questioning their sexuality. There have been cases where schools go to great lengths to promote the transitioning of a student's gender, such as having clothing (not usual for that child's biological gender) held at the school. Let's say it's a biological boy who goes to school, can change into a dress, put on make-up, and can be referred to by a new (feminine) name and, of course, with those "(in)appropriate" pronouns. When school is over for the day, that boy can take off his dress and make-up and get back into the clothes he wore when leaving his house that morning—all of which is hidden from his parents.

Other students who do not possess these gender identity issues and simply want to get a real education can become victims of this radical and dangerous agenda. These radical policies encourage and allow students to use the bathroom of their choosing at school. Gee, I wonder what kind of behavior goes on in those rooms. It's highly likely that drug use, sex, cheating, drinking, smoking, and even bullying goes on in there. To make matters worse, the policies prohibit adults from entering the bathrooms. That's right—there's zero supervision. Look what happened in Loudoun County, Virginia, where a young girl was sexually assaulted in the bathroom by a boy in a skirt. The school board was caught trying to hide this crime but to little or no avail.

Finally, the curtain has been pulled back on what is really being taught in our schools. We haven't even addressed what is going on in most of our colleges and universities. Yet I think if we can squish this nonsensical radical agenda of gender studies in the curricula (which can have devastating physical, psychological, and emotional results on an individual) and teach the truth about our history and bring back phonics and civics education, then students who go onto higher learning will be rooted in truth and be more equipped to discern what is taught at the college level.

Whether it is CRT, the 1619 Project, or gender-identity studies in schools, parents have had enough. They have been showing up at school board meetings across the country and voicing their alarm and disapproval of what is being taught and what is being hidden from parents. Some of the meetings have gotten loud yet are absent of the violence and destruction that the radical left protestors display when they want to voice a concern. But parents are now viewed as a threat and actually are being targeted as "Domestic Terrorists" by Attorney General Merrick Garland, Education Secretary Miguel Cordona (who allegedly solicited the National School Boards Association to write a letter to the Biden administration), and of course sleepy Joe himself. This administration is shifty, corrupt, and way too radical to hold the positions they do.

The disintegration of our educational system in America is not just the fault of the Biden administration, despite the fact that his first year in office has taken it to new lows. A huge milestone began in 1962 when the US Supreme Court banned prayer in schools. That's right; God was expelled from school. Public schools began in church buildings. The first school books were filled with Christian concepts and Bible verses. There has been a concerted effort to remove God from the classroom and public arena. The decision to remove prayer in schools was the foundation of the continued effort to remove any positive influence of God in schools and our nation. The school system has been in decline since they kicked out the Bible and prayer.

The primary objective of public education is to develop good moral citizens. Since the removal of prayer in schools in 1962, the divorce rate has tripled, the crime rate is off the charts, the number of abortions has dramatically increased, as has teen suicide and college entrance exam scores have dropped. Can we see a correlation here? Despite the legal edict to ban prayer in schools, students can and should still pray on their own and/or in small groups while at school

Yet the downfall and Marxist influence into our education system began early in the twentieth century. I strongly urge you to watch the five-part series on Fox Nation: *The MisEducation of America*. I would not do it justice to detail the horrific truth that this series reveals. Instead, please view it for yourselves.

There is a spark of hope. We have just begun to fight back (peacefully). We can no longer stand by and allow schools to inundate our children with hateful rhetoric, lead them into gender confusion, give students puberty blockers to alter their gender, lie about our history, and pass students to the next grade level or graduate them when their reading proficiency doesn't warrant these moves. After all, they are going to be our future leaders, teachers, DAs, judges, etc.

Get involved and thoroughly vet candidates at all levels of government, especially those running for your local school board. Attend school board meetings! Visit your child's class. Get engaged with their education at home. Or better yet, find an alternative to public schools such as a charter school, private school, home school, online school, parochial, or Christian school. As a reminder, all these alternatives should also be thoroughly vetted, as we must do with our elected officials. If public schools are going to continue to dumb down American children by the methods they are now employing, they will receive less funding when enrollment is decreased. It's highly likely that by choosing one of these options, you will have teachers that will do be committed to in-person learning and educate your child on the "3Rs" instead of the "3Hs."

God's Truth about Learning

As mentioned in chapter one, the Book of Proverbs is a spiritual recipe book designed to enable us to live successfully in relationship with God and the world He has created. The first chapter focuses on preparing a young person on how to deal with the challenges and responsibilities of adulthood and instructs parents on how to train their children.

> They teach wisdom and self-control; they will help you understand wise words. They will teach you how to be wise and self-controlled and will teach you to do what is honest and fair and right. They make the uneducated wise and give knowledge and sense to the young. Wise people can also listen and learn; even they can find good advice in these words. Then anyone can understand wise words and stories, the words of the wise and their riddles. Knowledge begins with respect for the LORD, but fools hate wisdom and discipline. My child, listen to your father's teaching and do not forget your mother's advice.
>
> Proverbs 1:1–8 (NCV)

People with wisdom have the skill to face life honestly and courageously and to manage it successfully so that God's purposes are fulfilled in their lives. It isn't enough simply to be educated and have knowledge, as important as education is. We also need wisdom, which is the ability to use knowledge and grasp the meaning of a situation, and understand what to do and how to handle it. If our current educators are flooding the minds of our children with hate, division, and unbiblical topics, then discernment is key for the parents, as well as the children.

"Jesus said to the people who believed in him, 'You are truly my disciples if you remain faithful to my teachings. And you will know the truth, and the truth will set you free'" (John 8:31, NLT). A disciple is a learner. And as we seek knowledge, we must exercise discernment so that what we learn will be truthful and righteous. Without truth, things start to fall apart. When people lie, the foundations of society begin to crumble. Whether it's a statement from a government official, a clause in a contract, a deposition in court, the media spreading misinformation or omitting real news, a teacher altering factual history, or a school not being transparent about the subject matter they are teaching, the truth cannot be violated without society ultimately suffering.

"For wisdom will enter your heart, and knowledge will fill
you with joy."
(Proverbs 2:10, NLT)

CHAPTER SIX

$---\S---$

The Crumbling of America –
Foreign Policy Disasters and Weakening Our Military

This quote from former Defense Secretary Robert Gates sums up the ineptitude of President Biden concerning our foreign policies. Gates wasn't kidding when he noted that Biden has "been wrong on nearly every major foreign policy and national security issue over the past four decades." It's amazing that someone who lacks wisdom, flip-flops on his position regarding situations with foreign countries, and operates with careless methods, can become our Commander in Chief.

Now, it's not only Biden who is operating in ways that put our national security at risk – it's the cast of clowns he has chosen for his administration. Let's take a look at a few of these far-left wackos. First, there is his Secretary of State, Antony Blinken. In 2002, Blinken served on the staff of then-Senator Biden, who supported the US invasion of Iraq. Blinken also supported an increased involvement in the Syria conflict, as well as being a staunch supporter of the armed intervention in Libya. We'll get to his failures as the current Secretary of State a bit later.

Then we have Biden's National Security Advisor, Jake Sullivan. His main focus has been his promotion of the Democrats' HR1 Bill and the voting rights legislation, claiming the failure to pass these radical proposals is a national security threat. Sullivan was a top aide to former Secretary of State Hillary Clinton and helped to orchestrate the disastrous military action in Libya that killed US Ambassador to Libya, Christopher Stevens. Sullivan, who played a key role in negotiating the failed Iran nuclear deal in 2015, is currently leading the Biden administration's efforts to revive that same controversial agreement, which the Trump administration had ended.

Prior to that, Sullivan was an advisor to Obama, who failed to enforce his "red line" on chemical weapons in Syria. Obama didn't do anything when the "red line" had been crossed, which had a domino effect. It changed Vladimir Putin's strategy regarding Russian military intervention in Ukraine. Once again, the United States took no significant action to deter Russian forces from destabilizing the country when annexing Crimea. And look where we are today with another threat to Ukraine by Russia.

There are other questionable characters in the Biden administration, but these two take the cake. General Mark Milley, Chairman of the Joint Chiefs of Staff, and Defense Secretary, Lloyd Austin. Let's start with Lloyd Austin. Prior to his retirement in 2016, Austin was the US Commander of Central Command, the headquarters for military operations in the Middle East and Afghanistan. As a rule, it is a bad idea to make any retired general the secretary of defense—a job expressly created for a civilian.

The principle of civilian control over the military is so ingrained in America's political culture that federal law barred officers from becoming defense secretaries within seven years of their retirement from the armed forces unless Congress passed a waiver allowing the exception. Guess what? The Senate approved the waiver in a 93-2 vote. The two senators who voted against the exception were Josh Hawley of Missouri and Mike Lee of Utah.

In 2015, Austin testified before the Senate Armed Services Committee to defend his dismal failure in dealing with ISIS. He told the Senate that the US continued to make progress against this Middle East terrorist organization. The late Senator, John McCain, came unglued and responded to Austin,

> I must say I've been a member of the committee for nearly thirty years, and I've never heard testimony like this. Basically, general, what you're telling us is that everything's fine as we see hundreds of thousands of refugees leave and flood Europe, as we're seeing now 250,000 Syrians slaughtered, as you see more and more Iranian control of the Shia militia. I have never seen a hearing that is as divorced from the reality of every outside expert.

It should be noted that in 2014, Austin told then-president Obama that the Islamic State was a "flash in the pan." He probably got that idea from his former boss (Obama), who once referred to ISIS as the "JV team."

Also, during this time, Austin's Central Command department was under internal investigation after whistleblowers said senior Central Command officials were doctoring intelligence reports to downplay the threat from ISIS. Fast forward to 2021, when Austin was not completely forthcoming regarding troop presence in Afghanistan during the disastrous and totally botched withdrawal in August. Who can we trust anymore?

Our military personnel is valued, respected, very much needed, and we honor them. So why are the military and political leadership trying so hard to make our military weaker and no longer a dominant force globally? Not only is Austin teaming up with Milley to make our military more "woke," he is making us weak by decreasing the number of troops through his reckless mandate forcing everyone in the armed forces must get the jab or face possible discharge. My goodness, the armed forces personnel are healthier than most of us.

Then, there's General Milley. He was a hold-over from the Trump administration, where he betrayed his Commander in Chief (Trump) by making secret calls to his counterpart in communist China, General Li Zuocheng. On October 30, 2020, Milley reportedly called Li to reassure him that the US military "is not going to attack or conduct any kinetic operations against you." Milley reportedly went so far as to tell Li that if then-President Donald Trump did order military action against China, "I'm going to call you ahead of time. It's not going to be a surprise."

Prior to that, during the heat of the violent, destructive, and fatal riots in the summer of 2020, Milley took it upon himself to rally other military leaders to help him undermine the Constitutional authority of the President of the United States (Trump). Milley was planning a strategy that would block any orders by Trump to use military force to handle the chaos in some American cities. Thankfully, Trump never had to go to those lengths. Trump should have fired him but didn't. This betrayer was kept on as Biden's Chairman of the Joint Chiefs of Betrayal and went on to bungle and weaken our military strength, as will be pointed out later.

While the Chinese military is preparing for war, the United States is putting all its efforts into becoming more "woke." The government's primary function is to protect its citizens. Being more concerned with diversity and domestic politics rather than the defense of the nation, and stressing racial quotas over preparedness and qualifications, won't keep America safe. Neither will emphasize critical race theory over military theory to keep us safe.

Milley, Austin, and Biden's other politicized generals are eroding the motive to fight by encouraging soldiers to embrace unpatriotic critical race theory and Black Lives Matter ideologies. Our military is devoted to protecting *all* lives because *all* lives matter! These radical, leftist, and flawed programs fail to strengthen our military. They are only weakening our effectiveness and destroying patriotic morale within the ranks—and the rest of the world is watching.

Speaking before the House Armed Services Committee on June 23, 2021, Milley defended teaching critical race theory to US Army cadets at West Point—and said it's important for those in uniform to understand "white rage." Milley stated that he is "widely read" in communist literature and, most notably, "I want to understand white rage, and I'm white." He went on to say, "I personally find it offensive that we are accusing the United States military or general officers are commissioned [and] noncommissioned officers of being 'woke,' or something else because we're studying some theories that are out there," Milley said. "I've read Karl Marx, I've read Lenin, that doesn't make me a communist." No, it makes you an idiot!

Biden and his bozo generals (Austin and Milley) were responsible for one of the most catastrophic, debilitating, and humiliating events in our nation's history—the disastrous withdrawal of the American military from Afghanistan. This twenty-year war with religious terrorists came to a tragic end on August 31, 2021, and is viewed as one of the lowest points for US foreign policy. Let's review the key points of the timeline for this horrific event:

• February 29, 2020—Under the Trump administration, the US and Taliban sign an agreement outlining the terms for a US withdrawal from Afghanistan by May 1, 2021. The agreement reads in part:

The United States is committed to withdraw from Afghanistan all military forces of the United States, its allies, and Coalition partners, including all non-diplomatic civilian personnel, private security contractors, trainers, advisors, and supporting services personnel within fourteen (14) months following announcement of this agreement, and will take the following measures in this regard.

• January 15, 2021 – The drawdown of troops in Afghanistan reached 2500. (This is Trump's last involvement with the withdrawal, as Biden was sworn in five days later.)

• March 25, 2021 – During a press conference at the White House (his one and only press conference in 2021), Biden said, "It's going to be hard to meet the May 1 deadline. Just in terms of tactical reasons, it's hard to get those troops out. If we leave, we're going to do so in a safe and orderly way." But he doesn't commit to an actual withdrawal date.

• April 14, 2021 – Biden declares that all troops would be removed from Afghanistan by September 11, 2021, and that withdrawal would *begin* on May 1, 2021. Biden said, "We will not conduct a hasty rush to the exit. We'll do it responsibly, deliberately, and safely." Biden added the US has "trained and equipped a standing force of over 300,000 Afghan personnel" and that "they'll continue to fight valiantly, on behalf of the Afghans, at great cost."

• July 6, 2021 – The US military confirmed that it had completely pulled out of Bagram Airfield, its largest airfield in Afghanistan. Oh, don't forget they left billions of dollars of military equipment as a parting gift to the terrorists who will be more than happy to use those same weapons against us, given the chance. I told you Biden and his generals, et al. are bozos!

• July 8, 2021 – Biden moves update for full troop withdrawal to August 31, stating, "Speed is safety."

• August 6, 2021 – The Taliban takes control of its first province, Nimroz – despite the agreement signed with the US in February of 2020.

• August 15, 2021 – Taliban fighters enter Kabul, the capital city of Afghanistan. The cowardly Afghan president Ghani flees the country. And similar to the disastrous withdrawal from Viet Nam in 1975, diplomats from the US embassy in Kabul are evacuated by helicopter.

• August 16, 2021 – Complete chaos in Kabul with citizens desperately trying to flee the city, including dozens and dozens of people clinging to departing American planes with several falling to their death. Speaking on Afghanistan for the first time in a week, Biden said the US had succeeded in weakening al-Qaida and that its goal was not to help establish democracy in Afghanistan. He also criticized the collapse of the Afghan military. But, nary a word about taking ownership for his decisions or role in this whole matter. Surprised? He hasn't taken responsibility for any of his failures, of which there are many.

• August 26, 2021 – As the chaos continued outside Kabul's International Airport, attempting to evacuate tens of thousands of (unvetted) Afghans and Americans, a suicide bombing takes place at the airport. The attack killed thirteen US service members, as well as nearly 200 Afghans, and injured hundreds more. ISIS-K claimed responsibility for this deadly attack.

• August 29, 2021 – The US conducted a drone strike targeting a *suspected* suicide bomber who allegedly posed an imminent threat to the Kabul airport. Tragically, the intelligence was wrong, and ten members of one family, including seven children, were killed.

In a rare case, General Austin actually owned up to this disaster. However, no military personnel would face disciplinary action for the deadly drone strike.

• August 30, 2021 – General Frank McKenzie, the commander of US Central Command, announced at the Pentagon that the last US military planes had left Afghanistan. The US departure marks the end of a fraught, chaotic, and bloody exit from the United States' longest war. McKenzie told reporters,

> The last C-17 lifted off from Hamid Karzai International Airport on August 30, this afternoon, at 3:29 p.m. East Coast time, and the last manned aircraft is now clearing the airspace above Afghanistan. There's a lot of heartbreak associated with this departure. We did not get everybody out that we wanted to get out.

Biden and his bungling buddies messed up big time in executing the disastrous withdrawal from Afghanistan. Not only did Biden keep switching the withdrawal date, but he also failed to follow his generals' advice about a troop presence. And not only did he fail to follow that advice, but he also denied he ever received that advice. He did so during a TV interview on August 23, 2021, with ABC's George Stephanopoulos. This was three days before the devasting deaths of thirteen service members by a suicide bomber. Biden lied, and people died!

How ludicrous it was to close Bagram Air Force Base. Whose idea was that? It was reported that Biden was so intent on reducing the number of troops to less than 1000 that a troop presence that small would not be able to secure a facility of that size. Then why didn't we keep enough troops to keep using that heavily-armed, remote facility, which was also equipped with an additional runway compared to that of the Kabul International Airport? Also, the facility could have housed and fed *legitimate* evacuees in an orderly manner rather than having them hang onto the wings of departing planes.

Not only did US troops desert Bagram in the dead of night, but they also abandoned billions of dollars of military weaponry, such as thirty-three Black Hawk helicopters and sixty-four thousand machine guns, which the Taliban was proudly donning after their takeover of Kabul.

By abandoning Bagram before the evacuating Americans and Afghans who assisted the US military all those years, the limited troop presence that was left was forced to guard the perimeter of the vulnerable and exposed Kabul International Airport—a deadly recipe for disaster. Not only has the US current leadership left behind countless numbers of Americans and green card holders et al., but the Biden administration also gave the Taliban a list of Americans and Afghans that the US wanted to get out of Afghanistan. Are you kidding?

This was a catastrophe of epic proportions and a blatant failure of policy and planning. Just think of what our European and other allies think about this. How much faith do they now have in America's ability to come to their aid if needed? You can guess what China, Russia, Iran, and North Korea are thinking. Our enemies see this botched withdrawal and the incompetence of our president and military leaders and are chomping at the bit to exploit it. Has anyone been held accountable? You know the answer to that.

Approximately ninety retired generals and admirals have signed a letter requesting that Secretary of Defense Lloyd Austin and the Chairman of the Joint Chiefs of Staff, General Mark Milley, resign from their positions. Part of that letter states, "The damage to the reputation of the United States is indescribable. We are now seen and will be seen for many years as an unreliable partner in any multinational agreement or operation. Trust in the United States is irreparably damaged." But, these two clowns would rather understand white rage, push CRT training, and kick people out of the military for not getting the jab that doesn't work—all while Uncle Joe shuffles off to an ice cream parlor.

Besides the Afghan debacle and the southern border crises that we have covered, Biden and his team of fools have had some other foreign policy doozies in his first year in office. After canceling the Keystone XL pipeline (as detailed in my first book), Biden gave his approval for the Nord Stream pipeline from Russia to Germany. And as our own domestic oil and gas production was stopped (which resulted in higher gas and heating prices), Biden begged OPEC and Russia to supply more oil and gas in hopes those prices would be reduced. Really? This must have been a joke, right?

Regarding China, Biden has had three or four phone calls with Chinese President Xi since taking office. Yet, he has failed to address the origins of the deadly China Virus, the military threat to Taiwan, China's increased presence in the South China Sea, or the Beijing Winter Olympics visa issues during these calls. Then what did they talk about? Blah, blah, blah! Oh, they probably discussed climate change (about which China is the biggest contributor to dirty air), or perhaps Xi wanted to send his best wishes to Hunter.

Speaking of China, who can forget when Secretary of State Antony Blinken and National Security Advisor Jake Sullivan attended a summit meeting in Alaska with China? Blinken and Sullivan wanted to address Hong Kong, Taiwan, cyber-attacks on the US, and human rights issues in Xinjiang with the Uyghur Muslims. The Chinese officials responded with a scolding of America and basically said that the US should stay out of China's internal and foreign affairs. Pointing to the Black Lives Matter movement, one Chinese diplomat stated, "We hope that the United States will do better on human rights; China has made steady progress in human rights." Blinken and Sullivan weren't expecting that. They don't expect much of anything in any situation, it seems.

And let's not forget when Biden blind-sided Australian President Morrison when they (Biden and Blinken) failed to inform and/or update Morrison about the troop withdrawal from Afghanistan. Australian troops had fought along with the US in the twenty-year war (where forty-three Australian soldiers had died). Blundering Biden/Blinken's failure to inform their ally about the final pull-out date is just another glaring example of foreign policy ineptitude.

This was also in concert with the fiasco about the cancellation by Australia of an important contract to buy submarines from France. It was revealed on September 15, 2021, that Australia had decided to make a deal with the US and the United Kingdom to purchase nuclear subs instead. Australia dumped France just hours before they announced a new alliance between Australia, the United Kingdom, and the United States (AUKUS).

Needless to say, France was incensed with all parties, but especially with the US. As a result of the snub France experienced, they decided to recall their ambassador to Washington for the first time since 1776. But here's the kicker. In an interview with a French TV station, our infamous "climate czar," John Kerry (you know, the one who actually destroys our climate by flying his private jet all over the world), admitted that sleepy Joe had no idea the French were angry about being duped. Kerry gingerly responded to the interviewer's question by saying,

He [Biden] asked me. He said, 'what's the situation?' and I explained exactly, uh he was he had not been aware of that, he literally, literally had not been aware of what had transpired. And I don't want to go into the details of it, but suffice it to say, that that the president, my president is very committed to, um, strengthening the relationship and making sure that this is a small event of the past and moving on to the much more important future.

We can only guess what Kerry actually meant. Either Biden didn't understand the ramifications of his actions or was told about what had happened and forgot, or his administration never told Biden in the first place, keeping him totally out of the loop. All three scenarios are very concerning that we have this president and his cronies in the White House. And don't you know how Kerry went to France? – his private jet!

And now we have tensions rising again between the US and Russia over Russia's military advance to take over Ukraine. In January 2022, Blinken met with his Russian counterpart and NATO to try to de-escalate the situation. Not much came out of that meeting. Things heated up with the serious threat of Russia invading Ukraine's capital city of Kyiv. The Biden administration says that US troops will not be fighting the Russians on Ukraine soil. But, the US has sent troops to neighboring countries to protect our NATO allies. Here we go again – getting involved in situations around the world. Oh, and of course, we will be sending millions of dollars in weapons to Ukraine. Hey Joe, here's an idea – or an afterthought. You should have given Ukraine at least half of the billions of dollars in weapons that you abandoned at Bagram Air Force Base in Afghanistan!

Russia has staged more than one hundred thousand troops on Ukraine's border since April of 2021. Russia is demanding that NATO change its mind about having Ukraine become a member of NATO (which was never on the table) and demanding that US troops' presence be removed from Eastern Europe and Central Asia. The US countered that by telling Russia there would be significant consequences should Russia invade Ukraine. Not sure if that would be in the form of economic sanctions or military action, or both. It's concerning that this tension has been elevated between US and Russia in light of the world's view that the US is one of a weak nation. And top it off, during Winter Olympics in Beijing, Putin and Xi declared they are now "best buds"—just what we needed!

Overall, it has been a dismal year for Biden and his administration—and we have a little less than three more years. Domestically we are a mess with sky-rocketing inflation, violent crime everywhere, rampant hate and divisiveness, failing schools are due to the woke teachers' union, blatant lies about the China Virus and how to handle it, a corrupt media, and the disregard for upholding our immigration laws to stop the mad influx of illegal aliens into our country—this is destroying America. But Biden's weak and dangerous approach to our foreign policies can have some catastrophic consequences. We all need to get on our knees and pray.

God's Truth on How to Govern and Lead

The Bible teaches that individuals and nations need to learn to obey God and depend on Him for guidance, blessing, safety, and understanding. When people lose their sense of values and reliance on God, bad things happen. The history of ancient Israel shows that war and oppression followed whenever they forgot God.

The United States is no exception to this timeless truth. God will not continue to bless a nation that no longer puts Him first, trusts Him, or obeys His laws. We need to pay attention to what God says, or we will suffer the consequences of poor decisions.

"Your own actions have brought this upon you. This punishment is bitter, piercing you to the heart!" (Jeremiah 4:18, NLT).

Throughout the Old Testament, we also see God dealing with Israel the same way a loving father deals with a child. When they willfully sinned against Him and began to worship idols or left Him out of their lives, God would chastise them. Sometimes, He would destroy them through the actions of other nations. Yet, each time He would deliver a remnant—once they had repented of their idolatry or disobedience. Let's hope it won't get to that point, and He won't completely give up on us.

"I am going to bring foreigners against you, the most ruthless of nations; they will draw their swords against your beauty and wisdom and pierce your shining splendor" (Ezekiel 28:7, NIV).

We certainly don't want to either become a huge weakness in the eyes of foreign nations, nor do we want to continue to enact careless policies that cause unnecessary damage and mistrust. It would be great if our leaders at all levels could follow the example of Daniel in the Bible. Daniel was a young man (probably in his teens) when he and others were captured and exiled to Babylon in 605 BC before the Babylonian King Nebuchadnezzar conquered and destroyed Jerusalem in 587 BC.

But Daniel was a devoted and obedient follower of God who never compromised his faith for any reason. His godly character and integrity resulted in a rise to prominence in leadership positions as advisors to the Babylonian kings, and subsequently, he became one of three top advisors under the Medo-Persian King,

Darius. Despite his co-workers having no belief in God, Daniel remained devoted to his faith and his daily prayer routine. Don't you think that if our leaders were more devoted to God and prayerfully sought His will in all decisions impacting our nation, we would be better off? That doesn't let us off the hook. We, too, must fervently pray for our nation and our leaders, regardless of what side of the aisle they come.

> Daniel soon proved himself more capable than all the other administrators and high officers. Because of Daniel's great ability, the king made plans to place him over the entire empire...He prayed three times a day, just as he had always done, giving thanks to his God.
>
> Daniel 6:3, 10 (NLT)

> "The wicked make evil plans against good people. They grind their teeth at them in anger. But the Lord laughs at the wicked because he sees that their day is coming."
> (Psalm 37:12–13, NCV)

CHAPTER SEVEN

$---\S---$

Voter Suppression Is a Myth — Voter Fraud Is a Reality

Even prior to the beginning of the Biden administration on January 20, 2020, the radical left Democrats have been unyielding in changing and controlling voting in America. It's highly likely that this crusade is to counter the fact that the Democrats are *done* in the upcoming elections in 2022 and 2024. They truly dodged a bullet in the 2020 election — they were caught cheating, but they weren't held accountable. Now they want to change all the rules to ensure they will be the party in power forever, despite not attaining or maintaining that power legitimately.

Regardless of political affiliation, elected officials and party leaders should put their financial ambitions aside and understand that election integrity is of critical importance in self-government and maintaining a functioning democratic republic. And voter fraud does not solely occur with Democrats — Republicans have been known to participate in these deceptive acts. Examples of voter fraud include altering of vote counts, impersonation fraud at the polls, ineligible voting, such as by illegal aliens, false voter registrations, duplicate voting, fraudulent absentee ballots, vote-buying, illegal assistance and intimidation of voters, electioneering while ballot harvesting, and mail-in ballots sent to deceased citizens that were subsequently completed by someone else. It was a dead giveaway in the 2020 election when some cities/states had received and counted more ballots than the number of registered voters in those particular jurisdictions. But, where was the accountability?

However, the Democrats aren't as concerned about voter fraud as they are about their ludicrous claim of "voter suppression." Okay, I may not be the sharpest knife in the drawer, but bumbling Biden stated the opposite during his address on the anniversary of the January 6 "Capitol riots" and during his vitriolic speech in Atlanta on January 10, 2022, to promote his voting rights bills. In both instances, he made this declaration, "The election of 2020 was the greatest demonstration of democracy in the history of this country. Over 150 million Americans went to the polls and voted that day. In a pandemic." Now, doesn't that deflate his claim that there is voter suppression? How can you have a record turn-out for voting and claim that voters are restrained from voting? The 2020 election featured the largest increase in voters on record (between two presidential elections), with 17 million more people voting in 2020 than in 2016. Here's the breakdown:

Non-Hispanic Whites: 71 percent voter turnout, compared to 65 percent in 2016

Hispanics: 54 percent, compared to 48 percent in 2016

Non-Hispanic Blacks: 63 percent, compared to 60 percent in 2016

Total number of Americans who voted in 2020: 159,633,396

Where's the suppression?

Still, nutty Nancy and crying Chuck have employed every trick to get two voting bills through the Senate. The "Freedom to Vote Act" and the "John Lewis Voting Rights Advancement Act" are two bills the radical left Democrats have tried to shove down the throats of Americans. These bills are scaled-back revisions of the HR1 legislation that Democrats couldn't get through the

Senate. These two bills should be wrapped into one bill called the "Freedom to Cheat in Elections Act."

The "Freedom to Vote Act" was an attempt by the radical left to federalize our elections. Thank God that this "attempt to cheat" bill didn't pass through the Senate. Here is a summary of what the "Freedom to Vote Act" was all about:

• Requires states to provide automatic voter registration, such as through the DMV,which means illegal aliens in at least fifteen states that allow illegal aliens to get a driver's license, would automatically be registered to vote.

• Requires states to provide online and same-day registration. This gives no time to verify if the voter is legit, but that's exactly what the Democrats want.

• It prohibits states from placing any restrictions or conditions on voters who want to vote absentee.

• Calls for making Election Day a national holiday. That's really not a bad idea if we reduce voting to one day.

• Forbids states from imposing voter ID requirements, except for first-time voters who register by mail.

• Prohibits notarization or witness signature requirements for mail-in voting.

When the Constitution was written, the Framers wanted to ensure that the federal government would restrain from having too much power and control over the states. The "Freedom to Vote Act" found its roots in Article 1, section 4 of the Constitution, which states, "The Times, Places and Manner of holding Elections for Senators and Representatives, shall be prescribed in each State by the Legislature thereof; but the Congress may at any time by Law make or alter such Regulations, except as to the Places of choosing Senators." However, this clause only applies to federal elections for the House and Senate. The Supreme Court ruled in 1892 that the Constitution leaves exclusively to the state legislature the management of presidential elections and insists that the state legislature's power cannot be relinquished or taken away.

Then there's the "John Lewis Voting Rights Advancement Act," which is the Democrats' attempt to increase federal oversight and take over all elections in the US. If passed, here is what this power-grabbing bill would do:

• It would make it legal in all states to conduct ballot harvesting. In other words, it would allow third-party individuals or groups to collect and submit ballots on another person's behalf. Gee, no chance for fraud there!

• States would need approval from the federal government in order for the states to make any changes to their election laws. So, if a state wanted to change the voting hours or change requirements for documents to prove identity, they would need to first have federal approval. Can you say over-reach?

• States would be penalized for imposing (what the radical Democrats consider) stringent voter ID measures. The Democrats feel that photo IDs showing proof of residency or proof of citizenship are burdensome and could lead to voter denial. Well, so are vaccine passports!

Several polls affirm that voter ID requirements are popular with all voters—Democrats, Republicans, and Independents (from all racial backgrounds). Besides the popularity of voter ID laws, the courts would likely uphold those laws requiring IDs if challenged. In 2021, at least eighteen states passed election reform laws to strengthen voter ID requirements and clear their voter registration rolls of the names of ineligible voters.

But, Biden, Harris, and the rest of the radical clown show continue to cry out that our current voter laws are an "attack on our democracy" and that they keep minorities from voting. Isn't it funny that Biden appointed cackling Kamala to be the "border czar" and then recently anointed her to lead the voter bill efforts—in other words, to make her the "voter fraud czar?" She did such a marvelous job at the border and, wouldn't you know it, performed equally as well trying to get the voting bills passed. How did Joe react? Ole Joe stated (in only his second full press conference since becoming president) that Harris would be his running mate in the 2024 presidential election. That's a gift from God!

If the Democrats want to ensure voter integrity, their proposals will do the complete opposite. And someone, please provide even one example of voter suppression. All these whining Democrats have failed to offer a crumb of evidence indicating that a *legitimate* voter has ever been denied their right to vote. So why have we been enduring this baloney for so long? Because *illegitimate* votes were counted in the last federal election, we ended up with these clowns in office. Lesson learned? I hope so!

But not to worry! The Democrats were not successful with the biggest trick in their bag—to end the filibuster. On January 19, 2022, the Democrats attempted and failed to scrap the filibuster rule, which requires sixty votes out of one hundred to end debate and proceed to vote on legislation. This is a major victory for conservatives and all Americans. Our elections will be conducted by Constitutional principles to maintain the protection, balance, and integrity of our election process.

Oh, the hypocrisy is still alive and well among the Democrats in Congress. It was as recent as 2017 when thirty Senate Democrats (including then-Senator Kamala Harris and Senator Chuck

Schumer) signed a bipartisan letter imploring Senate Majority Leader, Mitch McConnell, to keep the filibuster. On the flip side, in 2005, some Republicans brought up the idea to eliminate the filibuster. Their idea withered rather quickly. But the senators that protested the loudest against it were then-Senator Barack Obama, Senator Dianne Feinstein, Senator Chuck Schumer, and then-Senator Joe Biden.

In fact, at that time, Biden spoke on the floor of the Senate in opposition of ending the filibuster and said,

> Getting rid of the filibuster has long-term consequences. If there's one thing I've learned in my years here, once you change the rules and surrender the Senate's institutional power, you never get it back. And we're about to break the rules to change the rules...And I pray God, when the Democrats take back control, we don't make the kind of naked power grab you are doing.

Here's the kicker. All the while that the Democrats were desperate to end the filibuster, they actually used it on January 13, 2022 – that's right, six days before they had a vote to end the filibuster. Senator Ted Cruz wrote a bill that would have imposed sanctions on the construction of the Nord Stream 2 Pipeline in Russia. When Schumer discovered that some members of his party were in favor of Cruz's bill, he caved and allowed debate (filibuster) on the floor. Sadly, Cruz's bill failed by a vote of 54–44. So, Schumer allows a filibuster to defeat a bill at the same time he's trying to end the filibuster. The hypocrisy is amazing!

The truth is that the vast majority of Americans want election integrity. When the corrupt media squished the Hunter laptop story three weeks before the election, that was a glaring example of real election interference. And we are sick and tired of the claim that voter ID is "racist." For that matter, we're sick and tired of *everything* being referred to as "racist!" Nothing is more important than the sanctity of our election process; making it easier to vote and difficult to cheat benefits all Americans, regardless of political affiliation. We need to restore our faith in the election process — that is, after we restore our faith in God!

God's Truth about Integrity and Abuse of Power

If history has shown anything, it is that power corrupts fallen mankind; and absolute power absolutely corrupts. A nation or government may terminate the idea of God, but someone will take God's place in that government. That someone is most often an individual or group who begins to rule over its citizens and seeks to maintain their privileged position at all costs. This is why socialism has led to dictatorships so often in world history.

"You who love the LORD, hate evil! He protects the lives of his godly people and rescues them from the power of the wicked" (Psalm 97:10, NLT).

The ruthless and endless attempts that the far-left Democrats have been forcing to alter voting laws to ensure they remain in power for as long as they can are destroying our nation. What's more, is they have been doing it with deceptive measures. Their bills are stuffed into other bills, with countless pages that the majority of their colleagues will never read. Deep down, they know it is deception, but they don't care — and that is what makes it tragic.

But we have God on our side; if we so choose to lean completely on Him. He knows their tricks, and He knows the outcome of their corrupt schemes. We just need to trust that He is in control. It is for His purposes that these individuals are in power, but not for long. We must also do our part to look for the truth, share the truth with others, and vote accordingly for our future leaders. Oh, and always pray! God loves to hear from us.

"People with integrity walk safely, but those who follow
crooked paths will be exposed."
(Proverbs 10:9, NLT)

"The LORD detests people with crooked hearts, but he
delights in those with integrity. Evil people will surely be
punished, but the children of the godly will go free."
(Proverbs 11:20-21, NLT)

CHAPTER EIGHT

$- - -\S- - -$

Deception, Corruption, Lies, and Propaganda –
Our Government, Media, and Big Tech in Action

Propaganda is one of the most unnoticed and less spoken about tools that the far-left radicals, fake-news media, and social media companies are using to hood-wink Americans and slowly – or not so slowly, transform our Republic into a socialist/Marxist nation. The fingerprint of propaganda is that blatant lies are more useful and effective than the truth. Wake up; we're being "gaslighted"!

Now we can't blame all Democrats, most of whom are good Americans. But these are the voting folks who are isolated from honest, unbiased, and reliable sources of information about the actual events that are taking place in our communities, states, country, and world. As a *former* Democrat, I was also isolated from the truth because I got my news and information from liberal sources and friends. I think it was the socialist Obama-Care policy that was the beginning of my eyes being opened. True confession, I voted for Obama for his first term – then I got smart and changed parties. I broadened my social circle to include people with more conservative and rational perspectives, which eventually led to taking a more active role in truth-seeking. I was a late-bloomer to Christianity as well as conservatism, yet I'm so thankful to God for both.

So far in this book (as well as my previous book, *Our Crumbling Foundation – Will God Cancel Us?*) I have provided numerous examples of the deception, corruption, lies, and propaganda the radical left has poured on *we the people* for years. Propaganda is a tactic and staple of the left that is used by both the politician and the media. The goal is to drive people into competing camps and to manipulate people's thinking to gain political power. It is not based on fact but instead plays into the emotions of its targeted audience. And because they aren't committed to truth, main-street and social media giants label any viewpoint or position with which they disagree as "*misinformation.*" The result of which is usually in the form of "*canceling.*"

In 2021, the most blatant example of propagandizing Americans was the endless episodes of "*Fauci's farces.*" When people who are pathological liars start to feel the heat from those who challenge their proclamations, they resort to flip-flopping. Here's a run-down of a few of the many times "flip-flop Fauci" dictated his recommendations – all based on the science, of course.

• Early March of 2021, Fauci referred to lockdown measures in China as "*draconian*" and said that such restrictions wouldn't be "feasible" in the US.

• Five days later, he changed positions and said he was open to a national fourteen-day shutdown to help stop the spread.

• A month later, when a CNN interviewer questioned him on why social distancing and those stringent lockdowns weren't implemented sooner, he prompted confusion when he said, "There was a lot of pushback about shutting things down back then." But, wait a minute; wasn't he the one pushing back in the first place?

• In March of 2021, Fauci stated that there was "no reason" to wear a mask. By April, he changed his tune and has since drilled it into Americans that masks must be worn.

• In April of 2021, Fauci touted the use of remdesivir to treat COVID-19 (mind you, this was after only one clinical trial). He stated, "What it has proven is that a drug can block this virus." Now, there's a real scientist stating something is "proven" after only one clinical trial. As it turns out, the World Health Organization (WHO) and numerous doctors had advised against the use of remdesivir after it has caused severe kidney disease and death in many who had taken it.

• But all the while, Fauci has either been silent or dismissed the suggestion that other therapeutics (hydroxychloroquine and ivermectin) were effective in treating COVID-19. That's because they were way more affordable and had been proven to be safe and effective drugs for years. Oh, but then Fauci wouldn't receive the millions of dollars from big pharma like he has from pushing his poison.

Perhaps his biggest lie has been his denial that he was responsible for the funding of the gain-of-function research in the Wuhan lab. Of course, he lied to Congress about this (as well as millions of Americans), some who still think that his feces doesn't have an odor. This man should be criminally charged for his involvement in creating a deadly virus that has killed millions in the world, but you know that won't happen – at least while this administration is in charge. You probably have friends and family members who have not heard, seen, or even cared about these facts because the fake-news media and social media companies don't report or allow users to share the truth. So, it's left up to us to calmly and clearly help to open their eyes.

It wasn't only the "vaccine villain" who lied and flip-flopped. The CDC, WHO, NIH, and the FDA also joined in the reindeer games. And, of course, the misaligned media, Big Tech, and the radical leftists just added fuel to the fire with the constant barrage of false and fear-mongering reports. Again, COVID-19 was real, and yes, it was deadly to the vulnerable and already health-compromised individuals. But so is the flu.

These so-called scientific agencies either altered the truth, omitted the truth, or simply made up stories about COVID-19 to gain power and control over all people and/or reap monetary rewards — and they did it by using fear tactics and inaccurate statistics. They weren't following the science. If they had, the number of COVID-19 deaths would have been much lower than reported.

Lies were told by Fauci and his accomplices and fiercely propagated through the fake-news media and social media. One such example of truth-bending is in regards to the true and accurate number of deaths *from* COVID-19. From the start of COVID-19 until the end of 2021, the CDC has reported approximately 854,000 deaths *from* the virus. During the Trump administration, you would see the daily running death count displayed on television news. Since Biden took office, that is no longer the case. Perhaps it's because more people died under Biden's watch than Trump's.

Yet the question kept coming up as to whether people died *from* COVID-19 or *with* COVID-19. Well, we have now seen that fully-jabbed people get (and spread) the virus — more so than the un-jabbed, as it turns out. As a result, the CDC has been forced to shed some light on the truth. On January 9, 2022, during an interview with Bret Bair, CDC Director Rochelle Walensky stated,

In some hospitals that we've talked to, up to 40 percent of the patients who are coming in with COVID-19 are coming in not because they're sick with COVID-19, but because they're coming in with something else and have had to — COVID-19 or the omicron variant detected.

Then Baier asked her if she had a breakdown of all the deaths in the US, indicating how many were from COVID-19 as opposed to with COVID-19 and other comorbidities. Well, waffling Walensky dodged the answer by saying it takes weeks to collect the data (she was mainly referring to the omicron variant). It is likely that a large percentage of deaths from COVID-19 since its onset were people that died *with* the virus and not *from* the virus. Americans just want the truth. It is a fact that people with compromised immune systems, and those already suffering from respiratory diseases, obesity, diabetes, and other comorbidities, are the part of the population most at risk of death from COVID-19. But instead of putting all their efforts into protecting the at-risk population, Fauci et al. shut down the entire country; forced millions and millions to get jabs that have proven not to be as effective as their claims; and spent hours shame-basing Americans who did their research and decided what was best for them as individuals and opted not to get the jab, which has proven to be harmful to so many. And remember, it was Biden and Harris who, prior to the 2020 election, repeatedly declared they would *not* take the jab because they didn't trust it. So now they're in office, it's suddenly trustworthy?

Now the Biden administration has resorted to "big brother" tactics. It's insane that they want to fire people for not being vaxxed when the jab is becoming less effective each day. Do we really want to weaken the number of our military, our police, fire, first-responders, and healthcare workers — not from the virus, but from government overreach? With these people dismissed from their vital jobs, America is in real danger.

That's not the only "big brother" tactic this administration is employing. Now they are keeping a list of Americans who are requesting religious exemptions from COVID-19 jabs. On January 24, 2022, Republican members of Congress wrote a letter to Biden accusing him of targeting Americans seeking religious exemptions from the COVID-19 jab.

The Biden administration is testing out a policy in a small federal agency, the Pretrial Services Agency for the District of Columbia, that would likely serve as a model for government-assembled lists of Americans who object to the COVID-19 vaccines on religious grounds. The Pretrial Services Agency (PSA) is a federal government law-enforcement agency which is tasked with two main functions: gathering and presenting information about newly arrested defendants and available release options for use by a judicial officer in making decisions concerning a defendant's pretrial custody or release status. You don't think they will stop keeping records for just federal employees, do you? We're next! Our current government is spending time and money on tracking Americans requesting religious exemptions while other government officials place thousands and thousands of illegal aliens on buses and planes that take them to cities all over the country — free to roam without penalty. Give me a break — this is similar to Nazi Germany!

Well, enough about Fauci and the big brother government. Let's see how else the propaganda machine has been manipulating the minds of Americans. How about the January 6 insurrection hoax. Of course, it's just one of a string of hoaxes that the radical left has drummed up against Trump and other conservatives since 2015. Remember that was when the feds started spying on the Trump campaign in an attempt to get the goods on people close to him and eventually conduct a full-blown investigation on him and his administration.

The mainstream media, nutty Nancy, crying Chuck, shifty Schiff, and all the other leftist darlings were banging the drums loudly to go after Trump, all the while withholding the truth that the Democratic National Committee funded the manufactured Steele dossier that started the mess in the first place. Even the director of the FBI at the time, crooked Comey, knew the Democrats had paid for the made-up smear piece but denied it to Congress. Where's the accountability? Oh, there is none. Comey just went on to promote his book, which was also full of lies. It was Americans that had to suffer through the lengthy and extremely costly tax-payer funded investigations that ended up revealing that no Russian collusion on the part of Trump, or his administration, had taken place.

But the Democrats weren't done. Instead of doing the jobs they were elected to do, they spent their time going through not one but two impeachment fiascos. It didn't matter that American cities were literally being burned down by the ruthless radical-left mobs like BLM and Antifa. But of course, the fake-news media insisted they were "peaceful" protests, despite the fact that their months-long riots resulted in over $2 billion in property damage and claimed over twenty lives. This brings us to the final hoax before Trump left office — the January 6 insurrection hoax.

The dictionary defines an "insurrection" as "an act or instance of revolting against civil authority or an established government, or a violent attempt to take control of a government." Before we move on, let's be clear about what happened on January 6, 2021. Should a select group of protestors enter the Capitol building in the manner in which they did? No. Should they have entered the chamber floor? No. Should they have entered the offices of our elected representatives? No.

So, nobody is condoning the actions of those that took it upon themselves and/or were following marching orders they had received from some radical group to storm the Capitol building. But, the media, Biden, Harris, and Nancy's biased January 6 committee have been telling Americans a completely overblown and inaccurate account of what actually took place on that day.

Nancy's radical-left committee is made up of seven Democrats and two token left-leaning Republicans. This was after nutty Nancy blocked the appointments the House Minority Leader McCarthy had originally made. This goes against the House of Representatives' tradition where leaders of both parties appoint members to a committee with equal or proportional representation. But this is Nancy's swan song—her last hurrah at canceling conservatism and destroying Trump before she either retires or is voted out of office.

Now the liberal media will not focus on the fact that in August 2021, the FBI concluded its investigation of the January 6 attack on the Capitol and determined there was insufficient evidence to charge that the riot was an organized plot to overturn the presidential election results. Additionally, the FBI found no evidence that Trump, or people directly in Trump's circle, were involved in organizing the attack. They did, however, make arrests of people from far-right groups such as the Proud Boys and the Oath Keepers but stated that these groups did not have serious plans about what to do if they made it inside the capitol.

But that's not stopping nutty Nancy. Her committee of clowns is not just investigating the riot but investigating all the actions Trump, his administration, his legal team, and some Republican members of Congress may have done in an attempt to stop the certification of the election of Biden. The committee has subpoenaed countless individuals and their texts and emails, including Sean Hannity and Mark Meadows. But they won't look into the communications between nutty Nancy and her House Sergeant-at-Arms regarding his request to dispatch the National Guard and security preparedness in general (or lack thereof) on January 6 and the days leading up to it. It's pure hypocrisy!

One reason that Mark Meadows, former Chief of Staff for Trump, was subpoenaed as a result of the corrupt actions of shifty Adam Schiff. Schiff claimed to have obtained a copy of a text message from Meadows to former Vice President Pence instructing Pence to not certify the electoral votes from a handful of states. Just like when shifty Schiff claimed to have evidence against Trump in the Russian collusion hoax, he continued his shifty, lying tactics. This time he had doctored the text message and erased a key portion of the text. But he still presented it to Nancy's corrupt committee.

The original text message was from Joseph Schmitz, who is a Washington attorney and a former Department of Defense Inspector General. The text from Schmitz was originally sent to Ohio Representative Jim Jordan and included a four-page attachment detailing the constitutional authority the vice president of the Senate (Pence) had if he chose to object to the certification of the electoral votes submitted by the few states that had very questionable election results/practices. Jim Jordan then forwarded the text and attachment to Meadows.

Once again, shifty Schiff was wrong in his accusation and doctored evidence. In Schmitz's original text to Jordan, a portion of it read,

> On January 6, 2021, Vice President Mike Pence, as President of the Senate, should call out all the electoral votes that he believes are unconstitutional as no electoral votes at all – in accordance with guidance from founding father Alexander Hamilton and judicial precedence.

But ole shifty placed a period after the word "all" and erased the remainder of the sentence. In other words, it was like a directive to Pence to flat out not count some of the electoral votes. This never happened. It was just a sneaky attempt by shifty Schiff and his corrupt committee members to take down Trump.

There have been at least two well-done documentaries on what actually transpired on January 6, 2021. One was done by Tucker Carlsen on Fox Nation called *Patriot Surge*, a three-part series. And the other was produced by actor Nick Searcy (who happened to attend the rally for Trump on January 6) called *Capitol Punishment*. This can be found on the website https://capitolpunishmentthemovie.com. Yet, the committee certainly won't look at the facts these documentaries reveal.

So far, the clown committee has interviewed well over three hundred witnesses – behind closed doors, of course. Isn't it interesting that Nancy's corrupt committee will not release the over 14,000 hours of videotape from the Capitol police? What are they hiding? Oh, that's right – it's called the truth. There were small groups of organized rioters who planned disruption and possibly violence. But they used tens of thousands of actual peaceful patriots as cover for their unlawful antics. These militants broke into the East and West ends of the Capitol, smashing windows and doors. Once inside, they went upstairs. Some made it into the Senate chamber. On the other side of the building, a crowd of protestors attempted to smash through the doors of the House chamber. Regardless of the inexcusable actions of the ruthless protesters, the claims that Biden et al. spew about it being an "armed insurrection" are false. No guns were seized or used on that day, and no shots fired — that is except for one, the one that murdered Ashley Babbitt.

Ashley Babbitt was a former military police officer who served in both Iraq and Afghanistan. This unarmed protestor, unfortunately, attempted to climb into the smashed window of the House Chamber when a plain-clothed Capitol Police officer, Lt. Michael Byrd, fatally shot her. The media and the leftists falsely claimed that five people died in the "insurrection," including Capitol Police Officer Brian Sicknick, who allegedly was bludgeoned to death with a fire extinguisher.

Here's the truth about the five people who died at or near the Capitol, either on that same day or the following day. None of the deaths were caused by the protestors. Kevin Greeson died of heart disease on January 6. It was initially reported that Rosanne Boyland died when she was crushed by the stampede of protestors trying to break through the police line. But an autopsy later revealed an amphetamine overdose. Benjamin Philips died of heart disease on January 7. Despite the false claim that Officer Brian Sicknick had been killed at the riot, the truth is that he suffered two strokes the following day. The Chief Medical Examiner listed his death as "natural causes." And the fifth death was that of Ashley Babbitt. She was the only one *murdered* with a Glock 22 used by Lt. Byrd.

The DC police withheld the identity of Michael Byrd, an African-American Capitol Police officer who killed Babbitt, for eight months following the shooting. Normally, police departments are required to release the name of officers involved in fatal shootings within days of the incident. But since the US Capitol Police is controlled by and only answers to Congress, they don't "need no stinkin' rules" to follow. After all, crazy Nancy is in charge!

A little more about Mr. Byrd: This is not the first time Lt. Byrd has had an incident with his Glock 22. In February 2019, Byrd was identified as the Capitol Police officer who left his loaded service weapon (a Glock 22) unattended in a bathroom in the Capitol Visitor Center at the Capitol. He was the commander of the House Chambers section of the Capitol Police. Byrd told his colleagues the following day that he "will be treated differently" because of his rank as a lieutenant. What the heck is that supposed to imply? We don't know if any disciplinary action was taken because the US Capitol Police department does not disclose records on police misconduct. How convenient!

So, fast-forward to the fatal shooting with a Glock 22 on January 6. A half-baked investigation was conducted into the incident. When his identity was disclosed, Byrd appeared with NBC News anchor Lester Holt in August 2021, where he stated, "There's an investigative process [and] I was cleared by the DOJ [Department of Justice], and FBI and [the D.C.] Metropolitan Police," adding that the Capitol Police also cleared him of wrongdoing and decided not to discipline or demote him for the deadly shooting.

Investigations into the Byrd investigation reveal that he didn't provide any statement to investigators, and they didn't force him to make a statement. Byrd never swore under penalty of perjury his claim that he issued a fair warning to Babbitt before firing his weapon. Documents from eyewitnesses (including three other officers) reported they did not hear Byrd verbally warn Babbitt. Byrd did admit to Lester Holt that he never actually saw Babbitt brandish any weapon as she attempted to crawl through the broken window of the House Chamber. But regardless, he stated he felt threatened, and that is why he fatally shot an unarmed woman.

So Lt. Byrd is cleared and not charged with any violation/crime. Meanwhile, the feds have arrested at least 761 people as of January 24, 2022, for their involvement in the January 6 riot. The Sixth Amendment to the Constitution grants American citizens the right to a speedy trial. But some of the political prisoners of January 6 are still waiting to be brought to trial, some of whom have been kept in solitary confinement. The majority of the charges are for trespassing.

About one-fourth of the 700-plus arrests have resulted in guilty pleas, with 90 percent of those for misdemeanor offenses. Those who actually broke the law should be held accountable. But they should also get due process. Those whose actions were definitely reckless and negligent, like those of Byrd's, should also be held accountable. But wait a minute—sometimes they are.

Remember former Police Officer Kim Potter, who was found guilty of first and second-degree manslaughter charges in the accidental shooting death of Daunte Wright. She was recently sentenced to two years in prison for mistaking her tazer for her service weapon when Wright attempted to flee the scene of his arrest. Unlike Byrd, Potter verbally warned Wright with the words, "Tazer! Tazer! Tazer!" prior to shooting what she thought was her tazer. Yes, she should be held accountable for her negligence, but so should Byrd!

So, was the Capitol riot on January 6 an insurrection? Well, there was violence and some destruction to the building itself. But how would a group like that succeed in taking control of the government without being armed? Even the FBI concluded the radical rioters did not crash the Capitol with the intent to overthrow the government.

Yet, Biden, AOC, Nancy, Chuck, and the media call the events of January 6 a "threat to our democracy" and compare it with that of Pearl Harbor, 911, or the Civil War. And they claim that all those who attended the speech on January 6 are "domestic terrorists." Are you kidding? That is a complete insult to all those who gave their lives to defend our freedom, as well as all those (including first-responders) who lost their lives on 911 at the hands of *real* terrorists!

Hey Joe, Nancy, and all the other crazies on the left, here are examples of real domestic terrorism and/or insurrections. How about the Weather Underground bombing of the Capitol in 1971. By the way, that's the same group Chesa Boudin's (San Francisco District Attorney) parents joined and were later convicted in 1981 of an armored car robbery, but I digress. How about the 1995 bombing of the Alfred P. Murrah federal building in Oklahoma City, which killed 168 people. Timothy McVeigh and Terry Nichols were the radical right-wing terrorists responsible. It doesn't matter if you are on the left or the right; when you become radicalized and do horrendous acts such as this, you are a terrorist. January 6 was bad and regrettable, but it was not insurrection and was not terrorism. The only one actually killed was Ashely Babbitt, compared to the countless lives lost in the Civil War, 911, and Pearl Harbor. We'll just have to see where Nancy and her corrupt committee take us next. They need prayer, and so do we!

Twenty-twenty-one did have a couple of positive things about which we should take note. Two high-profile trials proved that our justice system (when done correctly) does work. The first case involved the horrific killing of Ahmaud Arbery, a twenty-five-year-old black man who was merely jogging in a neighborhood in Brunswick, Georgia, on February 23, 2021. Travis McMichael, his dad Gregory McMichael, and a neighbor William Bryan Jr.

were all convicted of felony murder. These three men chased down the jogging Arbery with their truck, were armed with a shotgun, and shot Arbery at close range. All of this was caught on videotape that was leaked two months after the murder. Justice was definitely served that day.

The other high-profile trial in 2021 also involved a fatal shooting. It was positive with respect to the verdict being reached on the actual facts of the case, in light of the uproar across America. Kyle Rittenhouse, the then seventeen-year-old, was accused of killing two protesters and injuring a third during riots in Kenosha, Wisconsin. While the trial was taking place, the media coverage, the biased opinions voiced by Biden, Harris, Cori Bush, Maxine Waters, and numerous other politicians et al. were downright shameful. They all described Rittenhouse as being a white supremacist, despite the fact that the three men he shot in self-defense were white.

They demonized Rittenhouse and threw the presumption of innocence until proven guilty completely out the window. Of course, they focused solely on their racialized ideologies and failed to actually watch the trial and see the facts—the truth. Thank God that the jury members were committed to doing their civic duty as jurors by basing their findings on the truth. Rittenhouse was found not guilty, but his life will never be the same.

This chapter could go on and on because there are infinite examples of deception, corruption, lies, and propaganda that have taken place just in the last few years. But from what has been shared in these pages, you get the idea of the slippery slope on which we now find ourselves as a republic. Now that our eyes are open, and with God's help, let's move into action to restore our republic. "Those who will not be governed by God will be ruled by tyrants" (William Penn).

God's Truth about Deception, Corruption, Lies, and Propaganda
The Bible is full of examples of when the Israelites turned away from God and worshipped idols. Their disobedience to God and His loving wisdom and guidance through His commands would result in God having to cast judgment and consequence for their actions. God spoke through His prophet Jeremiah and warned of coming judgment.

"'They use their tongues like a bow, shooting lies from their mouths like arrows. Lies, not truth, have grown strong in the land. They go from one evil thing to another. They do not know who I am,' says the LORD" (Jeremiah 9:3, NCV).

We live in a treacherous world, with lies and deceptions sprinkled about like land mines that are hidden from view. Satan is the *"father of lies"* (John 8:44) and works his evilness into the hearts of those who have taken their eyes off of God. You can bet that Satan is working overtime in our world today because of our independence from God. We need to listen to our heavenly Father. Return to Him, and He will return to us.

"Listen to me! For I have important things to tell you. Everything I say is right, for I speak the truth and detest every kind of deception" (Proverbs 8:6–7, NLT).

It's sad that so many of our so-called leaders, as well as corporate and social media goons, spend so much effort into avoiding, denying, withholding, and distorting the truth about almost everything. Ronald Regan made popular the phrase "Trust, but verify" in the 1980s. But it is probably wiser during these turbulent times to "verify, then trust" to ensure you are getting the truth.

"Evil people don't understand justice, but those who follow
the Lord understand completely."
(Proverbs 28:5, NLT)

CHAPTER NINE
−−−§−−−

Let's Take a Stand — God's Way

The plan was to gracefully write this final chapter from a place of providing hope and inspiration to take back our God and our country. Before that, however, the world is spinning at warp speed, and notable events are occurring each day — it's hard to keep up with all that's happening. So, I would be remiss if I didn't include some very recent updates to what has been shared in the previous chapters. Okay, here's a brief rundown of what's taken place in the last few days:

• The Biden administration has sent US troops to European NATO countries that border Ukraine because Russia has officially invaded Ukraine. Putin's power and pride have led to this senseless act of war, where thousands of lives are at risk. Thankfully, the Nord Stream 2 Pipeline has been paused, but that won't stop the out-of-control prices we've been paying (and will continue to pay) for gas and oil. Perhaps if Biden hadn't recklessly ended our energy independence by shutting down the Keystone Pipeline, America wouldn't have had to get as involved in the disputes between other countries. If we can't protect our own borders and properly manage the affairs in our own country, what on earth are we doing involving ourselves with the affairs and border concerns of other countries? We can't continue to be the world's police! Let's not forget that China is looming large!

• Speaking of borders, the December 2021 number of encounters with illegal aliens at our southern border increased to 178,840 — compared to 73,994 in December of 2020. There were 153,941 encounters just in January of 2022. Nobody in the Biden administration, including our illustrious "border czar" cacklin' Harris, is doing a thing about it — except illegal things.

• Those illegal things include recent video reports showing dozens of single (mostly adult male) migrants being shuttled from a make-shift processing center in downtown Brownsville, Texas, to a local airport for flights to various cities in the US. These flights are done in the middle of the night and are done on private chartered flights paid for by US taxpayers. The federal government also signed a $36 million deal with a private security firm, MVM, to transport these illegal aliens (many of whom have criminal records) all over our nation.

• Republican Congresswoman from New York, Claudia Tenney, told Fox News on January 27, 2022, the following,

> This is a complete, aggravated dereliction of duty, which is why last night on Twitter, I called for Joe Biden to be impeached and removed. His primary obligation as the commander-in-chief and president of the United States is to enforce our laws, to live up to his oath, to enforce our border security, and to tell the truth to the American people.

Yeah, this "lying dog-faced pony soldier" probably should be impeached!

• Oh, here's one you will love. The eighty-one-year-old Speaker of the House, nutty Nancy, announced on January 25, 2022, that she will be running for re-election in 2022. Now, she's not running for the money—heaven knows she doesn't need that since she and her husband Paul raked in over $30 million last year in very conveniently-timed stock trades, but that's another story. Nancy said she was running (hold on) "for the children." She announced on Twitter, "Thank you for giving me the privilege to represent our city and our San Francisco values in the Congress. Human rights, reproductive justice, LGBTQ equality, respect for immigrants, and care for each other," Pelosi said. "When people ask me, 'what are the three most important issues facing the Congress?' I always say the same thing: Our children. Our children. Our children," she added. "That is my why. Why I am in Congress—for the children," she continued, "This is my story. And this is my song. As you hear me say, 'When you're in the arena, you have to be able to take a punch or throw a punch for the children." Now, if that doesn't bring a tear to your eye, I don't know what will. Besides being the most dangerous speaker in history, she's also entertaining!

• As usual, the radical left uses Big Tech to do the dirty work the federal government can't do—censor political opponents. In September 2021, the Federal Elections Commission cleared Twitter of violating any election laws by censoring a report by the New York Post (less than three weeks before the 2020 election) regarding Hunter Biden's disgusting laptop. Many Democrats have expressed that if they had been made aware of that story, they wouldn't have voted for Biden. But again, the maniac media and Big Tech control many elected minions. In an effort to again squish the voices of conservatives and withhold the truth, YouTube just permanently banned Fox News host Dan Bongino for posting a video saying that masks are useless against COVID-19. And the hits just keep on coming!

• This is chilling. The number of police officers shot in the line of duty in 2021 is the highest on record. The Federal Order of Police reported that in 2021 there were 346 officers were shot—63 of whom were killed. They also reported that there were 95 ambush-style attacks. Just in January 2022, two New York City officers were shot and killed, a Bronx, New York, officer was shot and wounded while responding to report of a disturbance, two officers were shot and wounded in Ferguson, Montana, a Houston, Texas, police officer was ambushed and killed during a routine traffic stop (by the way, the shooter was an illegal alien), and four days later three more Houston police officers were shot and wounded. To make matters worse, most of these killings took place in cities with ultra-liberal and/or Soros-backed District Attorneys, so guess how much accountability will be imposed? Probably none.

• Remember in the previous chapter that exposed more government take-over with the federal Pretrial Services Agency's (PSA) plan to record personal religious information of employees with religious accommodation requests for those seeking religious exception from all the federally-mandated vaccination requirements? Well, wouldn't you know it—eighteen other government agencies are planning to make religious-objector lists too. But one agency has taken it up a huge notch. The Commerce Department is now going to keep a list of all federal employees seeking a "medical exemption" from Biden's draconian jab mandate for all federal employees. Again, we're next!

• Okay, here's the last one, or this book will never end. Remember the long-awaited Durham Report? Well, it is nearing completion. On February 11, 2022, Special Counsel John Durham disclosed in a court filing that alleges that Hillary Clinton's 2016 campaign hired a tech company to obtain data from servers at Trump Tower and later the White House. Let's call it what it really is—spying! This cyber-security company wanted to extract whatever dirt they thought they could dig up to support their false narrative about the now-debunked claim that Trump and Russia were in cahoots. This is just the beginning. The door is widening for more indictments to come down exposing the criminal activity of Clinton and her band of thugs. "If you set a trap for others, you will get caught in it yourself" (Proverbs 26:27, NLT).

I'm sure by now you are either completely frustrated or have given up completely on America—I hope not. But I do hope you are frustrated enough to do something about it. You might be thinking, *I'm only one person; what could I possibly do to change the state of our nation?*

Well, gather with some like-minded friends/family and see what the possibilities are. A famous American cultural anthropologist, Margaret Mead, says, "Never doubt that a small group of thoughtful, committed citizens can change the world. Indeed, it is the only thing that ever has."

Included in an earlier chapter was a Bible verse from chapter 13 of the Book of Romans where the Apostle Paul wrote, "The authorities that exist have been established by God" (Romans 13:1, NIV). Now, you don't think God just puts leaders in position and then walks away—also expecting us to do absolutely nothing. Perhaps He places corrupt leaders in positions of power to grab our attention to the fact that we need God in our lives. Whatever the case, we cannot remain idle when we are being led down a ruthless, tyrannical, and evil path. So, what should we do?

Well, for starters, we need to acknowledge that we might have failed to do our part to truly vet and understand who we (or others) have elected into their positions of leadership. Here's a little test. Can you name the members of your City Council, County Commission, State Assembly, State Senate, US Congressional, or US Senate representatives? Can you name your city/state district attorney, Lt. governor, governor, the US attorney general, the vice president, or the president? I'm sure you could name that last two!

The point is, as concerned citizens of this amazing country, we might not be as "in-tune" as we'd like to think. Many of us [myself included] spend a lot of time griping about our elected officials. But besides voting, we have done squat to ensure that the spread of the radical-left socialist agenda stops. Now's the time!

There's reason for hope. Americans are starting to wake up to see for themselves what is really going on. Despite COVID-19 having wreaked havoc on the world, there has been a silver lining. *We the people* are beginning to push back on the jab mandates, and parents are pushing back on the mask mandates for children, unnecessary remote learning, and Marxist curriculum. Just look at what happened in Virginia—a blue state. This can be the beginning of something great. We can shrink our government's power-grab and grow in our freedom.

We are in a very important election year (aren't they all?). If you failed to name even one-third of your elected representatives from the previous list, you (and I) need to get to work. Start putting some real effort into vetting the candidates. Find out if they are all lip-service and no action. Find out where they stand on moral values. Find out if they have a track record of actually getting things accomplished. And, it doesn't matter to which party they belong. They could be a registered Democrat—but if their policies, principles, and plans are realistic, fiscally-conservative, and for the betterment of America, then vote for them. We must do our homework!

And once you finally get to know the names of your elected representatives (whether you voted for them or not), communicate with them. Perhaps our emails, letters, or texts written to our reps don't always reach them because they are first screened or poo-pooed by staff members—but keep at it. Write letters of encouragement when they are legislating in ways that support the greater good of Americans, or you can write letters clearly stating your opposition (and why) to their support of legislation that leads us down an ugly trail. You can do this as individuals or get together with others to brainstorm and craft letters from more than one voice.

It is challenging when we have good friends and/or family members who have completely opposite views on America, values, and laws than we have. Again, this is mainly a result of the truth being withheld by the malicious media and Big Tech. So, here's something you might try. If and when you engage in a peaceful discussion about politics (there's an oxymoron), here are two pretty powerful questions you can ask your liberal-minded friend or family member.

• The first question is: *What are you afraid conservatives and their policies might do to our country?*

Most likely, they will respond by saying, "I'm afraid we'll have Trump, or someone like him leading our country with racist tweets and actions." Well, besides the fact that tweets don't actually move the needle on what happens in our country, you might respond by highlighting all of the actual policies, executive orders, and accomplishments that truly benefitted our nation when a patriotic conservative was in the White House, here are just a few:

secure borders	low unemployment
stronger military	improved trade agreements
energy independence	right-to-try (for terminally ill)
no inflation	keeping China and North Korea in check
lower taxes	reduction in illegal alien encounters
businesses returning to America	enhancing veteran care
prison reform	reduced worthless government regulations
opportunity zones	ended "catch and release"
ISIS caliphate defeated	crackdown on MS-13 gangs
record low-unemployment minorities	decline in prescription drug prices
record manufacturing jobs added	increase in economic growth

Now you notice that those accomplishments from conservative leadership were unlike the radical liberal policies and executive orders that have been thrust upon America in the last year. These conservative accomplishments from the previous administration moved America forward, our nation prospered, our nation was protected, and the lives of Americans of all races were improved. And then COVID-19 hit. But, the Trump administration did not fold like a rusty old lawn chair. We struggled, but we held on. The real collapse came on January 20, 2021. The leftist policies were all about "taking away" stuff, like the Keystone Pipeline; our freedom to choose if we wanted a dangerous jab to be injected into our bodies, our children's right to have in-person learning, and keeping the unnecessary mandates on businesses and the general public, which resulted in our economy going down the drain; and keeping lists on people who don't do what they say and threatening to peek into our private financial activity. So, here's the second question you can ask your liberal friends/family members — it's a powerful one!

• *What conservative policy or leadership action has actually impacted you in a negative way?*

My guess is that it will be difficult for anyone to come up with a legitimate answer. I strongly urge you to give this a try. The primary purpose in writing this book (as well as my previous one) is and was to get the truth out to as many people as possible — particularly those to whom the truth has been withheld.

Secondly, since we are only beginning to wake up and realize the damage that has been done in the past year by this feckless administration, my other purpose is to motivate all of us to get involved and do something about it. We must put all our efforts into restoring our republic because our life (as we know it) depends on it. "Those who expect to reap the blessings of freedom must, like men, undergo the fatigue of supporting it" (Thomas Paine).

Please forgive me — I'm going to repeat some of the ideas I included in my previous book about actual steps we can employ to do our patriotic duty to take back our country. It first starts with prayer. A Holocaust survivor and true hero, Corri Ten Boom, once asked, "Is prayer your steering wheel or your spare tire?"

Prayer should drive us daily and be our go-to in all our circumstances and decisions — not just in times of desperation or when our tire is flat. Wouldn't you rather have God, Who knows you like no other, to be your Advisor in life? So, we need to pray for our nation, pray for our leaders (it doesn't matter if they have a "D" or "R" in front of their name), and pray for wisdom, discernment, and courage to get involved with saving our nation.

Read the Constitution! Our Constitution was not just intended for those who lived nearly 250 years ago. It was intended for all generations since its beginning. The Constitution helps to regulate the relationship between the government and the people in such a manner that no one part can abuse their power in any way possible. It guarantees the protection of the most basic rights such as the right to life, the right to freedom (religion, speech, peaceful assembly), the right to property, the right to bear arms, and the right to participate freely in the democratic system.

When an administration is getting out of hand and bending the guidelines of the Constitution, we need to actually know what the Constitution says in order to realize when it is being violated. And we won't make that realization if we haven't read it.

In addition to the previously mentioned importance of knowing who your representatives are and thoroughly vetting those running for office, it's imperative to attend your local City Council and/or County Commission meetings. And, as you can see the damage done to our schools and education as a whole in the past number of years, it is imperative to attend your local School Board meetings. I repeat: it's imperative! Also, it's important to invest your time into volunteering for a political campaign and/or as an election worker. If we are there to watch the process, we can shout very loudly if and when we see election fraud. If we're sitting on our couch, we can only watch the results of an election on TV.

God's Truth about America

This brings us to the cornerstone of all of this—our Creator! From time to time, God will place us in situations to test our allegiance to Him—a time such as this. How does God change a situation, a problem, or an outcome? He uses men and women—His created ones. In the Old Testament, God used Moses to deliver His people from Egypt. He used Ester to prevent the evil slaughter of Jews. He used the Apostle Paul (formerly a persecutor of early Christians) to preach and convert thousands and thousands of people to Christianity.

Often in the Old Testament, prophets (those whom God chose to speak through) would be mocked and ignored by God's chosen people—the Jews. One such prophet was Micah. He warned the people that because they had turned from God and had sinned so greatly, God would send His judgment. First, he warned the leaders about their corrupt ways and about false prophets who gave false security to the people by telling them, "Don't worry, nothing will happen to you."

"I said, 'Listen, you leaders of Israel! You are supposed to know right from wrong, but you are the very ones who hate good and love evil—You hate justice and twist all that is right'"(Micah 3:1-2, 9, NLT).

"Your leaders exchange justice for bribes. Your priests teach for a price. Your prophets tell the future for money. But they rely on the Lord when they say, 'After all, the Lord is with us. Nothing bad will happen to us'" (Micah 3:11, GW).

But Micah believed God when He warned that Israel would fall to Assyria, which happened in 721 BC, and that the Babylonians would take the Jews into exile and destroy Jerusalem, which happened between 606-586 BC. I imagine that God's patience is wearing thin with our leaders and with us. It's time to return to Him; team up with Him, and have Him lead us to victory! There's still hope.

> But there's also this, it's not too late — God's personal Message! — 'Come back to me and really mean it! Come fasting and weeping, sorry for your sins!' Change your life, not just your clothes. Come back to God, your God. And here's why: God is kind and merciful. He takes a deep breath, puts up with a lot, this most patient God, extravagant in love, always ready to cancel catastrophe. Who knows? Maybe he'll do it now, maybe he'll turn around and show pity. Maybe, when all's said and done, there'll be blessings full and robust for your God!
>
> Joel 2:12-14 (MSG)

So how do we return to God and our Christian roots? Remember, we were a Christian nation upon our founding. When we read the Founder's own writings, we can see their moral positions at the time. One such writing is from a former president, John Adams, in 1798 states:

> The safety and prosperity of nations ultimately and essentially depend on the protection and blessing of Almighty God; and the national acknowledgment of this truth is not only an indispensable duty, which the people owe to him, but a duty whose natural influence is favorable to the promotion of that morality and piety, without which social happiness cannot exist, nor the blessings of a free government be enjoyed.

Are you ready? We can do this! Let's be truth-seekers and truth-sharers. Get informed, get involved. And remember, we can't do this alone. We absolutely need to trust and lean on God through all that we do. It starts with prayer — if God heard and answered the prayers of Daniel, He will certainly hear and answer ours. God bless you, and God bless America!

$$--- \S ---$$

Then he said, 'Don't be afraid, Daniel. Since the first day you began to pray for understanding and to humble yourself before your God, your request has been heard in heaven. I have come in answer to your prayer.'

Daniel 10:12 (NLT)

ABOUT THE AUTHOR

– –§– –

      Mist Carter is a retired corporate manager who became a Christian patriot following retirement. In fact, she gave her life to Christ thirty thousand feet above ground in an airplane, perhaps so she could be closer to heaven from the get-go. God quickly gifted her with a talent to write and lead women's Bible studies. She found that the frequent discussions with friends and family about politics and the state of our nation were not really doing anything to improve the situation. So she decided to write a book of truth hope, and action. She loves God, her country, family, friends, and golf.

www.ingramcontent.com/pod-product-compliance
Lightning Source LLC
Chambersburg PA
CBHW060237030426
42335CB00014B/1494